Prisoner Without A Crime

A Memoir
by
Jack Jennings

PRISONER WITHOUT A CRIME

First Published 2011
This Edition Published 2016

ISBN: 978-1-4709-6110-7

Printed and bound by Lulu.com

Contents

Foreword

One evening, in the autumn of 1993, Dad sat down and started writing about the early years of his life – a couple of months later he had completed these memoirs.

Before this event my father rarely spoke of his war-time experiences. It was, and still is, a painful experience for him. However, writing his memories was a cathartic experience for him and he is now more willing to speak of his experiences.

Since writing his story, he has undertaken three return trips to Singapore and Thailand – firstly with his older daughter, Hazel, in 1995, then with me, his other daughter, in 2005. As a result, the memoirs were amended, with an Epilogue and Appendices added, in 2006 and a small number of copies were printed and bound for close family members. With the publication of this book in mind, Dad added a further Epilogue following his third return to Singapore and Thailand in 2010 – this time being accompanied by his grand-daughter, Carolyn. I'm sure that Dad would like to join me in thanking my husband Paul, for his help in putting all the elements of this book together and bringing it to fruition.

What makes this account so compelling is that the words used are exactly as they were written by my father. There is no ghost writer which results in a stark, straightforward telling of his story. There may be inaccuracies but one has to bear in mind that this story was not put to paper until fifty years after the events recalled. For clarity, a time-line has been included in the Appendices – dates that Dad was unable to pinpoint accurately in his original story have been identified using other documents and the Internet.

In writing these memoirs, which were intended primarily for his family, Dad assumed a certain knowledge. For clarity it is worth mentioning that places referred to in his early life are in the *Black*

Country of the West Midlands – an area to the north and west of (but not inclusive of) Birmingham and to the south and east of Wolverhampton.

At the unveiling of the FEPOW Repatriation Memorial, Liverpool Pier Head. October 15th 2011

Dad still attends many of the Far East Prisoner-Of-War (FEPOW) events that take place throughout the country. Many people who lost loved-ones during and after their internment by the Japanese are grateful for his insights into what life was like during that terrible time. He has been featured quite frequently in local newspapers, both in the Black Country and more recently in Torbay, where he now lives.

He has given illustrated talks to primary school children who have been studying the second world war and is particularly moved by their enthusiasm to learn from his experiences.

Through an organisation called COFEPOW (Children and Families of Far East Prisoners-of-War), we have made a number of new

iv

friends and realise that my sister and I are the lucky ones - Dad came home. We are both immensely proud of him.

Carol Barrett

November 2011

Introduction to this Edition

Since the original publication of Jack's memoirs in 2011 it has become necessary to update them.

A third Epilogue has been added, detailing Jacks fourth return to Thailand and Singapore in 2015.

In addition to this, further information has come to light which has enabled me to update the timeline (*Appendix 8*) and add some footnotes to Jack's narrative.

I would like to thank Rod Beattie and his team at the Thailand-Burma Railway Centre for the additional information about Jack's time in Thailand. The research undertaken by Jon Cooper in Singapore has also enabled more detail to be added to the *Battle for Singapore* section of the book.

For those with a particular interest in the 1st Battalion of the Cambridgeshires, I can recommend the following books (all of which were used in the research for this edition of the book):

Kept – the Other Side of Tenko	*L.L. Baynes*
A Line of Lost Lives	*J. Clayton*
Battalion at War	*Michael Moore*
Tigers in the Park	*Jon Cooper*

The former two books were written by Cambridgeshire veterans. Michael Moore is Sgt Moore's son – the book was compiled from his father's diary. Jon's book is a result of his extensive archaeological work in Singapore and draws on the other books, as well as this book.

Paul Barrett

April 2016

The First Ten Years 1919 – 1929

It is not easy to look back on one's life after seventy-three years and try to put together the story directly from memory without the useful possession of diaries. This, then, is the story of my life as I remember it, which may be interesting to my family or anyone else.

I was born on the tenth of March 1919 in a terraced house near to Old Hill Church, when at that time the roof was stripped off and was being repaired. This, I suppose, gave me an early start in life to enjoy the fresh air. In those days the houses were built with cast-iron open firegrates in bedrooms and downstairs rooms, but the only occasion when a fire was lit in the bedrooms was if someone was ill. The reason in our case was that we could not afford the cost of coal to that extent.

The main room downstairs had a firegrate with side oven, which was very good for cooking, providing someone was able to attend to it and keep a good fire going. But this had to be kept clean, so we had no fire, thus no heating until this was laboriously cleaned with black lead to make it shine. The coal was delivered in loads of a ton or more in front of the house and on the road. This then had to be carried in buckets, tin baths or arms to the back of the house to the coalhouse. As soon as you were old enough and in all weathers this job had to be done by all children and mothers; fathers, of course, were working.

The lavatory was away from the back of the house where all waste products dropped into the soil pit which was emptied occasionally by council workmen, wheeled and dumped on the road, and loaded onto carts. This was generally done very early in the morning. Eventually this was converted to a W.C. when I was about five years old.

The back yard was shared by four houses which was typical of this type of terraced houses in the street. Therefore the children all played in groups, in one open area, generally having a good time. The parents of these families, generally, were good friends, most having similar work and hobbies. Some kept pigs, others kept chickens, pigeons, cats or dogs, and so there was lots to talk about amongst parents, together, after work or at weekends. We lived in this house with my grandparents, aunt and cousin, so, with my parents and two sisters, that made nine in all to share three bedrooms. We had a lively upbringing. Another brother died at the age of five, who I never knew, and a sister died at the age of two, who I just remember.

I began school at the local infants' school when I was five. This school was only a short distance from the house, and I attended there until I was between eight and nine. The only thing that has remained in my memory while there, was one day when I was smacked on the arm when the boy next to me told the teacher that I had bobbed out my tongue to her. This was not so, as I was only moistening my dry lips, as I was no doubt waiting for our free milk which we had at playtime. My playmates duly sorted out the informer when we went out at playtime.

I was seven years old at the time of the 1926 General Strike and I remember picking coal from the railroad which ran along the end of the street. The track was raided every time a train passed, little pieces of coal being jolted off. We filled our buckets quickly and ran off home before the policeman caught us. The police station was very close to our house, so there were always policemen not far away.

My mother had worked before having children at the nearby foundry works, and was accused with others of playing pranks on their blind employer, such as placing obstacles in the way for him to fall over. Several years later when I was eight years old, it was the common daily sight to see this former employer of my mother walk back from the works at lunchtime to his home about a mile away. His habit was to walk in the middle of the road. It was very rare for motor vehicles to pass through our street, so a motor horn from behind could scare anyone. So on seeing blind Solomon coming up the street, I and others occasionally crept up behind and made a bad imitation noise of a motor horn. This of course made old Sol' jump sideways and wait for the passing car which never came. This happened once too many times for him to endure and being close to our house he turned and came to see my mother, asking for her by her maiden name. My mother was absolutely dumbstruck when he said it was her son who was responsible for playing tricks on him. With carefully chosen words to Sol' from my mother, and a few threatening words to me, the episode was forgotten and not repeated.

There were many hawkers around the streets in those days, all with either a handcart or a horse and cart. Besides the bread cart, the milk cart came daily with milk sold right out of the churns. There was ice cream sold in a wafer, cornet, or a tea cup. The scrap man came occasionally with a cart fitted with a roundabout. For some scrap you could have a ride. Another visitor was the ironmonger, with everything on his cart from a candle, to saucepans, a bucket or a bath. Then there was the salt lady who brought huge blocks of salt to sell. The grocer who was blind came with all the provisions in the food line. There was a scissor grinder, and a line prop dealer, a fishmonger and a chimney sweep, just to name a few. The only trouble was that most people were not very well off.

It was about this time, when I was eight, that I had to change schools. This school was in the opposite direction, and just a bit further away. I stayed at this school for about two years. My only memory of note was taking a mirror to school to sketch my own portrait. My effort was not much of a likeness. From then on I loved to play football whenever I could. My father had a wooden scooter made for me by the carpenter at his work, which gave me lots of pleasure until it wore out. Then I was fortunate enough to have a treadle scooter given to me by my mother's domestic employer. This was a big improvement, as it only required the treadle to be pressed and released to propel it along, the back wheel being turned by engaging a ratchet wheel. It was a pleasure trip to go on errands on that scooter.

Other hobbies were collecting cigarette cards to make a set of fifty. The subjects were birds, animals, football players, film stars and many more. I still remember the many film stars, although I rarely went to the cinema. Marbles in different designs were also collected. We played games with our marbles which we called *Chuck in the hole* or *Shoot the ring*. Both games were played to win or lose more marbles. With the cigarette cards our game of *Picture or Print* required one to call which side of the card would land uppermost when flipped into the air by your opponent. Again, they were won or lost, so it was luck that decided how long it took to get a set. In the warmer weather we played cricket, hopscotch, skipping or rounders. My mother never saw much of me as long as I could play outdoors.

My father at this time was gravely ill with cancer, and after a lot of medication and nursing he died when I was only eight. This was a great loss to my mother, my sisters and I. My mother was left to struggle to keep us, but that she did quite well, working very hard. It was a real setback for our education because we could no longer afford any books.

In the school summer holiday my mother took us to the hopfields near Worcester to pick hops. We used to stay three or four weeks on this working holiday. The farmer paid a few pence for each basket picked, so we helped a little until we became tired, but mother carried on working until five o'clock. Not being very much help as a hop picker my mother sent me back to the farmyard to light the fire for the evening meal. After the meal there was very little to do so most pickers went back to the barn sleeping quarters to talk or have a sing song. Men, women and children all slept on the floor close together. It was really a rough and tough life, but everyone seemed to enjoy it and felt better for it, going back year after year.

The second ten years 1929 – 1939

When I was ten I was moved to an intermediate school about a mile away. This was a long way to walk back home at lunchtime. Sometimes a few of us lads would come out of school and wait for a slow lorry or steam engine to come out of the nearby rail goods yard. We would then chase after it and hang from the tail board for dear life until we were closer to home. We then had to wait for the wagon to slow down for us to release our grip, and make a safe return to earth. We got to know which wagon was going our way.

My mother took in a lot of washing to do for a few people. In those days she had a wooden washing tub and a wooden dolly. The water was heated in a brick surrounded cast iron boiler over a coal fire, and then ladled into the tub, with clothes to wash and a few handfuls of powder. Then the clothes were pounded with the dolly in an already steamy wash-house for about ten minutes. When considered clean enough they were put through the mangle with big six inch rollers. When the pressure was put on the mangle, it was hard work to turn the eighteen inch diameter wheel to squeeze the water out. This pounding, and turning the mangle, was what I was given to do on wash days when I came home to my lunch from school. My mother would say, "Here Jack, come and do this while I get your dinner." Then when the washing was finished and ironed, my sister and I would have to take it back to where it came from. That could be as much as a mile away, on foot of course.

At the intermediate school I remember we had someone come to give us a talk on the Ovaltine product, which was a kind of advertising gimmick. Afterwards we had to write an essay on the subject. There were three prizes for the best essays and I was the winner of the second prize, which was Ovaltine samples and Ovaltine chocolate. This success inspired me to do well in the entrance exam for a

5

chance to go to the Central Higher Grade school, in which I succeeded. So at eleven years old I changed schools again. I enjoyed my time at this school, always going early in the morning especially to have the privilege of ringing the bell, as was usual for a short while before classes began.

I now had my first bicycle which came in handy to hurry to and from school. My friends also had bicycles, so during the summer months we organised outings together at weekends to the local beauty spots. We took sandwiches, and bat and ball, to really have a good day out. Sometimes we cycled fifteen or more miles each way, enjoying ourselves in the fresh air.

It was about this time that my mother was offered a key to a new house. This was quite exciting, so my sisters and I went to see where we were likely to be going to live. With our encouragement my mother accepted the key and we soon moved into the new house away from grandparents, aunt and cousin. The distance to school was very much the same as before but in a different direction. It was a pleasure to come from school to the new house where I was able to do homework in comfort. We had a large lounge, kitchen, bathroom and coal store downstairs, and three bedrooms, but now we also had a lovely big garden. The garden entailed a lot of hard work over a long period before it was dug over and planted. My mother became a keen gardener. My friend had a nice garden with an archway and trellis work on either side about three feet in height. With roses growing along each side of the trellis and over the archway it gave the garden a bit of character. It gave me the idea to ask my mother if we could have one. When I had the offer of help from my friend, my mother agreed to let me do the job. I found this very interesting and challenging, as my knowledge of woodwork then was very little. With my friend's help we slowly assembled the archway and trellis and erected it along the back of the house. Then we had to paint it green to complete the job. The next job was to buy and plant the climbing and rambling roses, which was done with much satisfaction. The follow on job from that was to lay a brick path from the archway to the bottom of the garden. This was a hard but essential job but when completed our garden began to take shape. There, I think, my gardening enthusiasm ended. It was my mother who became the gardener.

In the 1930s, and even a few years before then, I attended Sunday School every Sunday morning and afternoon, and also the adjoining Methodist Chapel in the morning and evening. There were some very good teachers at the Sunday school who organised Scripture and Band of Hope classes. They taught us that life could be good without wrongdoing and drinking alcohol. There was also a Boys Club and Girl Guides for the girls, which were attended enthusiastically. We entered into scripture examinations with other schools and also temperance exams from which I gained several book prizes. At the Boys Club we learnt plays and produced them on stage in the schoolroom. One such play has remained in my memory because it was so popular. We performed this play called *The Nigger Parliament* many times and at different locations. It was about an all black Negro parliament debating, and a very funny comedy it was. The words were often wrongly or strangely pronounced. The word "political" became "politickle."

Following on from this I was asked to join a Drama Group with a senior cast who were rehearsing for Shakespeare's *Merry Wives of Windsor*. I got the part of Robin, and attended rehearsals every week. After many weeks the play was ready to go on stage. We had the dress rehearsal, and then at the final moment the producer fell ill. As she was taking two parts, and no-one could take over, it was abruptly cancelled. This ended my stage career.

As I entered my teens the next thing that I did was to join the local cricket club as a member. This allowed me to watch the first and second team play at Haden Hill ground. It also enabled me to practice in the nets and sometimes with the team members on the ground. My love of cricket grew from this early age, and I still like to watch a match. In my late teens, I did the scoring for Old Hill second team in the Birmingham League, which I enjoyed very much.

At the age of fourteen, although I was happy to continue school, my mother wanted me to leave and get work, to help run the home. One

7

could leave at fourteen then, or at our school, carry on to eighteen. So my mother arranged an interview for an office trainee at Dudley. This was not successful. In a short time after that a friend of my mother's suggested I should try the joinery works where her son was working. Not very thrilled at this kind of work, I was urged to go and try my luck. This time I was offered a job in the joinery shop to start after the spring holiday, or two months after my fourteenth birthday. It was a very hard job working at the rear end of a four cutter moulding machine. My job was collecting the lengths of mouldings as they came through, tying them in bundles and taking them to the timber storage racks. After that batch came through, I had to get the timber in from the stacks, enough to do the next type of moulding, and then help to saw it to size to go through the machine again.

After twelve months at this work I was moved to a bench job to assist a tradesman making purpose made joinery. There were fourteen such pairs of workers who between them turned out a lot of work. Now I was beginning to like my job, so then I enrolled for evening classes twice a week doing cabinet work. This was at Dudley Art College, so after working until five-thirty, it meant hurrying back home, washing and changing, and having a meal. Then a long walk, about a mile and a half to catch the bus to Dudley for classes from seven thirty until nine o'clock. By the time I was home it was bedtime and I was very tired. This was continued until I was called to join the Army at the start of the Second World War in 1939. During that time at college I had made by hand, and to my own designs, a chest of drawers and my own bedroom suite in oak, all French polished, all of which remains my bedroom suite today.

The hours of work were from seven till five in winter, and seven till six in summer, except the two nights when I was allowed to finish at five-thirty for evening classes. Nevertheless, at every possible moment of spare time I made stools with a woven seagrass seat, and sold them to relatives and friends for a small profit. Many other woodwork jobs were made for neighbours whenever I had spare time. All the wood and other materials for making my bedroom suite which I have mentioned before were bought a little at a time. They were first of all taken home, and then I had to take them on the bus to Dudley Art School. I was no more than sixteen when I made my own workshed and erected it in the garden. Then I made a workbench. The timber for this I remember purchasing from my workplace, balancing the lot on my bicycle across the saddle and handlebars, and with one foot on the pedal I rode most of the way home. It was mainly a steady slope, downwards of course. The shed came in very useful and remained there until I married, then it was moved to our future home. In 1957 I sold the shed when we moved to a new house, my present home. The bench was taken to the new house; it was reduced but is still in use today in 1993.

It was at the age of seventeen when I began what was to become a serious friendship with a girlfriend, Mary, whom I had known for several years by going to Sunday School. We used to meet with other boys and girls around the lamppost after homework was done, laughing, joking, and telling yarns during the dark winter months. In the summer we walked to the local park to meet up and have a game together or listen to the band. Then, one Sunday after Chapel we met by the park and took our first walk together. After that Sunday walk we became very good friends, meeting on free evenings and weekends, whenever possible.

The following spring holiday we decided to go hiking for the day. We took a packed lunch and set off about 9.30 a.m. from her home in Old Hill. After walking approximately three miles in the direction of Bromsgrove out in the countryside, a car came alongside, stopped, and the driver enquired if we would like a lift. We turned to each other to consider the offer, but we answered "No thanks, we are only out hiking."

The man said, "How far are you going?"

I said, "Probably as far as the Lickey Hills."

He replied, "I am going to Austins' work, that's in your direction if you wish to come." Thinking it would give us the opportunity to go farther afield on our hike, we took up the challenge. So we sped to Austins' work, arriving quite early. Thanking him for the lift, we then continued our walk, thinking that we could now venture further; but

9

we didn't have a map, so we had to remember the signs so as to find our way back home. We carried on walking until about mid-day. By this time we were close to Redditch where we found a nice spot to have our lunch. Little did we realize as we sat talking that we had three or four hours walking plus the time it would take to cover the distance we rode in the car. So on this lovely sunny holiday afternoon we began our very long walk back home. Talking and walking without a care in the world, and following the same route as our outward journey, we loved every minute. Mile after mile and hour after hour we walked which was pleasant until the sun went down, reminding us that it was getting late. At that point our attention was drawn to our tired feet, but we still had a long way to get home. Naturally, no car stopped to give us a lift now, and we were not on a bus route. On and on we walked, evermore tired and footsore, walking more slowly all the time. At last at about nine o'clock we arrived back at Mary's home. We enjoyed our day out very much, but we suffered with sore feet next day. On our next meeting Mary said she couldn't bear the clothes on her feet that night, they were so sore. So much for our hiking day, we must have walked well over twenty miles.

Cycling was still a great love of mine, and at work there were other enthusiasts. One workmate, who was a few years older than me, had a tandem bicycle. He went on quite long trips with his wife on this tandem, and it came as a surprise when he asked me if I wished to go with him on the back of the tandem, to the cyclists' Annual Meeting at Meridon near Coventry. Because I had never ridden on a tandem before, on this particular Sunday we set off early to be in time for the morning service beginning at eleven o'clock. It was roughly twenty six miles each way so there was ample time for me to get accustomed to this machine. I found it a very enjoyable experience, and I have never seen so many cyclists together.

At this time in my life, still courting strongly with my girlfriend Mary, we began to go to the theatre. Neither of us had much pocket money so we had to save hard to be able to enjoy our new found pleasure.

Besides going to the local theatre to see Musicals, we occasionally went to Birmingham Hippodrome to see top stars of the day in Variety Shows. We saw many of the old favourites like Tommy Trinder, Max Miller, Randolph Sutton, Larry Adler, Florrie Ford, and others. It is a love of the theatre and music, and especially good singing, that has remained with us. Another kind of music which we loved to hear was played by brass bands in the local park regularly every Sunday in the summer. Haden Hill was then, and still is, a lovely park. There must have been thousands there on a Sunday to walk around, and listen to the band, and I must stress at this point that there was never any misbehaviour. The park to us had everything to enjoy oneself. With natural lakes and trees, historic buildings, and bowling greens, and tennis courts, it was a great attraction for all ages. We spent some of the happiest days of our lives there.

Another summer pastime which I enjoyed was rowing. Ednam, the friend who helped me with the garden trellis, took me rowing for the first time. He was an easy-going, quiet but well-spoken character. The place where we rowed was a picturesque, disused stretch of canal and was so peaceful. It was two or three miles walk from home, or a short bike ride. Each time I went my technique improved as each backward stroke produced a satisfying skimming sound across the surface of the water. Other friends sometimes went with me and later Mary came too, when I persuaded her that I was capable. On a warm sunny day it was most enjoyable, giving that lovely feeling of time well spent.

Cycling at the age of nineteen had a special appeal when I had a brand new, shining chrome, bicycle. It had hub brakes and dynamo lighting. My excursions into the countryside were more enjoyable and more frequent. There was at this time a workmate who enjoyed riding, so we planned to go in the summer holidays on our cycles to the seaside for a week's holiday. The nearest resort was Weston-Super-Mare. This also happened to be where my girlfriend Mary was going with her uncle, aunt, and cousin. It was decided that we go on this holiday to Weston, which was an extremely long journey of 108 miles.

We started at three-thirty in the morning on quiet, dark roads, progressing steadily. As we rode, we gradually witnessed the dawn come up and the birds started their dawn chorus. It was the start of a beautiful sunny day and continued to be an unforgettable, gorgeous day. We had a few stops along the way, and finally arrived at the seafront at about two o'clock in the afternoon. We found accommodation at a guest house, although we had to accept a small chalet in the garden for sleeping. It was a most enjoyable week. The food was good and the other guests in the house who also came from the Midlands were most friendly. My friend knew of course how eager I was to see my girlfriend during the week, so it was arranged between us for me to go out with her one day. The weekend came all too quickly with another ride back home; another 108 miles. Luckily it was lovely weather again, but it seemed much harder and longer going back. We had of course only the Sunday to get over it, because we were back at work on Monday morning.

Soon afterwards that same year I spotted an advert in the local newspaper. It was asking for anyone who would be interested in joining up to form a harmonica band. I had been playing one since I was about six years old and I thought it sounded quite interesting. On Saturday afternoon off I went to the meeting place at Brierley Hill. The organiser played an accordion and he was looking for about five more to join the band. He had the required number apply that day, so the band was formed and rehearsals began with four mouth organ players, an accordionist and a drummer. Afterwards we met every Saturday afternoon and learnt many pieces of music. Many weeks later we were able to put on a concert at a local school. We each wore grey flannel trousers with a wide, pleated, dark blue silk waistband, a white shirt and blue and white striped tie. Bookings were few but we continued practising.

About the same time I enrolled for a Correspondence course for Carpentry and Joinery. With evening classes twice a week I was very busy outside working hours. After about fifteen months doing the Correspondence course I had to give it up, mainly because I couldn't afford the monthly instalments. My mother could not or would not help me either.

Now at twenty, I had finished making the wardrobe at evening classes, to complete the bedroom suite. It was now at home in my bedroom where I could see the satisfying result of five years patient work, all done by hand. I was rewarded each year with a prize and a free studentship as well.

Conscription

In June that year, 1939, due to the deteriorating European crisis, I was called for conscription into the Army.

A state of nerves existed in the country as preparation for war with Germany continued. I was loaned out to another builder, to put blackouts up to skylights and windows of the Drill Hall at Halesowen which belonged to the Worcestershire Regiment. I did further work making cellars more bomb proof by adding stout timbers to the ceilings under the shops in the High Street of Lye.

On Sunday the third of September, we waited for an important announcement to be made on Radio by the Prime Minister, Neville Chamberlain. The announcement said, "We are at war with Germany." The first militia was called up for a few weeks training then shipped to France to join the regular army units. The blackouts to every house and factory were put up with as much speed as possible. Car lights were diffused and ration books and clothing coupons issued.

A few weeks later I received my calling up papers with the second militia intake. I had to report to Chelmsford barracks on the twentieth of October. A railway warrant was issued for the journey. The train from Old Hill to Birmingham was packed with hundreds of young men bound for duty in the Armed Forces, a few of whom I knew. At Birmingham the station was packed with men who all seemed to have a similar destination.

At Chelmsford we were taken from the station to the sorting depot, for me it was the barracks. I was allocated to the infantry battalion attached to the Suffolk Regiment, namely the First Battalion of the Cambridgeshire Regiment. Others were distributed to the other East Anglian Regiments. I was taken to Cambridge with many local lads whom I knew or had made friends with on the journey. After a meal in the drill hall at Cambridge, we paired off to be taken around to the house where we were to be billeted. Next day we were fitted out with army clothes wherever possible. Two lads couldn't get fitted up, one was six foot five and thin, the other little more than five feet tall and tubby. They had to drill in plain clothes for a while except for a khaki hat.

We did eight weeks of intensive drilling and marching, also weapon training with rifle and machine guns. We practised firing in the drill hall and on the rifle range. At the end of that training we were taken to join the main body of the battalion at Weeting Hall in Brandon, Norfolk. The large hall, secluded in the quiet countryside of Norfolk, was an ideal place for us to live and train. The grounds were lovely, but it was so isolated from any outside pleasure. There was nowhere to go in the spare time that we had.

The Headquarter Company of the Battalion, of which I was a member, was stationed at Weeting Hall and the four companies (A,B,C, and D) which formed the battalion were stationed within a few miles of us. The batch of men to join the Headquarter Company were split up into different sections, i.e. the platoons of mortars, cooks, signals, transport, gun carriers, medicals, headquarters and pioneers. The pioneers were made up of different tradesmen, plus water carriers and sanitary men. I was one of six carpenters, who altogether made about twenty men. Our job was clear: to assist, make or repair anything required for the company's needs. Because of this we were excused many parades, drills, and marches. Even so, we did quite a lot as the training became intensive, especially when we linked up with the companies for a manoeuvre. The accommodation and food were good, as was the NAFFI in the grounds. I was able to write home to say how much I enjoyed the life. Time went by so quickly and it was Christmas before we knew it. I think we had a week's leave.

In the New Year I was selected to go on a carpenters' course in London. It was on a cold day in winter, after the details had been sorted out, that I was driven to the local railway station in an open tourer car. The driver had to race against time through the country lanes, in order for me to catch the train.

16

Arriving at London I had to go by tube train to Highbury. The Northern Polytechnic College where I had to go was opposite the station. Other soldiers from different Regiments were there to enrol. We were put into groups and taken to our accommodation for the course. I was in a room with three others at the Cumberland Hotel in Highbury Grove. With me were two men from Scotland and one from Birmingham. All the meals at the hotel were taken with other civilian residents, served by nice young ladies from Yorkshire. We walked to the College and back each day. The day usually began with one hour of P.T. in the gymnasium. The instructor was a very fit man of about sixty who showed us how unfit we really were. Each day, after P.T., we did woodwork joints from blue-prints, or technical drawing. The weekend was free time; therefore we could either go home for a weekend or discover London. There was no-one to give us orders, so we were free as civilians but we still had to wear a uniform.

On one occasion when I went home, together with the room-mate who came from Birmingham, the trains on the journey back to London were held up. The Germans had dropped bombs around in raids on the city. It made us arrive late and by that time there was no transport back to Highbury. We enquired from a policeman what we could do. He suggested that we have a night at the Police station. There was little alternative as it was so late, so he led us on to get a night's sleep. It turned out to be Scotland Yard station where we were shown to a cell and given blankets. Next morning we awoke to the sound of tinkling tea cups. We washed and dressed, then hurried into the dining room to be given breakfast. Thanking them for their help, we quickly left. We arrived back in Highbury in time to go to College. Our room-mates wouldn't believe us when we told them where we had spent the night.

There were about eight of us soldiers in the hotel. The four of us in my room usually got on well together. We talked to the residents in the dining room and lounge and made good friends. One lady, who was alone, kindly asked us if we would like to have supper at her flat which was more in the centre of London. We agreed to go one evening at the weekend. It seemed unusual for one woman to be asking several soldiers to her flat, and we wondered what we had let ourselves in for. On arrival we were led upstairs to her room and invited to take a seat. It was a bed-sit room. She offered us a drink then brought out the food (lots of assorted titbits) which we enjoyed as we talked away, with a few jokes here and there. She couldn't have been nicer. She was good company and a lovely person who was genuinely trying to be kind to the forces.

The Windmill Theatre never closed during the war, but we never went anyway. For one thing we couldn't afford it. We often went to the snooker or billiard halls to pass away an evening. Sometimes we went to a forces club for a drink and a game of chess. It was there that I first learnt how to play the game, which I enjoyed. There wasn't anything in the hotel to pass the time away at night, only talk or perhaps a card game. On one occasion we started to throw pillows at one another. The room was an oblong shape with two single beds along the two side walls. The two Scots were in opposite corners and we two Midlanders were in the other corners. It started when one Scot threw a pillow in a friendly manner for the opposite man to catch. Then it developed into a game of catching the pillow in turns. It hotted up as pillows flew across the room to make catching more difficult. That didn't last long until the two fiery Scots lost their tempers. One threw a pillow so hard that in trying to avoid the full force, the other hit his head on the end of the bed. It split his forehead which began bleeding badly. Luckily there was a hospital nearby where he had to go to have it stitched, accompanied by his adversary. It was late at night then, but at half past midnight they still hadn't returned so we went out to look for them. A hundred yards up the road was a mobile fish and chip shop where we stopped to get some chips. Before we had finished eating them on the way to the hospital, along came our room-mates, one wounded, but both the best of pals. It was one o'clock in the morning when we got to bed.

As the course progressed I was getting very fit with regular daily gymnasium exercises. In the first few months of the year we played some football in the park at weekends. Later on, several of us were able to play cricket and form a team to represent the college. One match I played in was against a team whose ground was at West Ham. I loved to play cricket, and at that time it was army life at its best. The carpenters' course at the college was also going well, but the fact was that it was only for six months. Thankfully I had escaped the winter in a bleak Norfolk countryside and the army routine. It was summer again but I didn't know what the future had in store. We had our exams and I was pleased with my work. The instructors were pleased with the results too. They said we would all be promoted when we returned to our units.

One thing was for sure, it was going to be a tougher life from now on. The British Expeditionary Forces had been forced to be evacuated from Dunkirk beaches, in the greatest escape and rescue operation ever. We had to go back and prepare for anything.

Back in Brandon at the end of a travel weary journey from London, I reported to *H.Q. Company Office*. This was quite strange, because when I gave details of my absence to the sergeant-major, it seemed as if they had completely forgotten about me. The thought entered my mind as to whether I should have bothered to go back. I knew I was in the army again the next day; back to the strict routine: early morning reveille, breakfast, on parade and the usual fatigues or jobs around the billets.

The war had been going on now for six months or more. We had experienced lots of air raids all over the country, and in France, our troops were under severe pressure and were fast losing territory, resulting in the evacuation from Dunkirk. The threat of invasion by the Germans now put us more on the alert. Therefore the whole battalion was split up and moved to various places in Norfolk[1]. Our company moved to Wymondham for a short time, then North Walsham and quite soon to the coast at Happisburgh. Here we prepared for possible invasion plans. A lot of hard work making pill boxes took place.

One such occasion I remember so well. After constructing a pill-box or look-out, which the sergeant had detailed us to build against the

---

1   The move to Norfolk occurred on 1ˢᵗ July, 1940.

side of a brick farm building, I was detailed to camouflage it. The usual camouflage in the army was to conceal guns or gun emplacements with imitation foliage. The idea of making this look-out post resemble a tree didn't seem correct to me, being a brick wall and an oblong shape. Therefore I painted it to blend in with the wall. When I finished I stepped back a few paces to admire my handiwork. Just then the sergeant came back to see the results of my artwork.

The sergeant was a tall, very strong well-built man, who was a stonemason by trade. He had a round red face, but instead of being feared he was a bit of a softie. The other N.C.O.s would often pull his leg and were highly amused when he talked, as he occasionally used a big word but a wrong one.

His cheerful face changed as he turned away from me to look at the camouflaged post. At the sight of the extension to the building, instead of a 'tree', his cheeks puffed out getting redder. He exploded, "What do you think this is?" He immediately picked up the paint and brush and splashed green and brown patches of paint all over, in true army style. "That's what I wanted," he said, and walked away in anger. To me it looked more obviously like what it was: a disguised look-out post!

Every two or three nights a week we took guard, two hours on, four hours off. I was on guard one night, busily looking out across the sea for lights or any movement, listening and looking all around the post. It was a cold, quiet, dark night. Suddenly the approaching footsteps got too close for comfort. I challenged the intruder, shouting "Halt and give the password!"

The answer came back with a swear word. "That's ....it, it's Captain Coulson. What is the password?"

I then called, "Advance Captain Coulson". With a few exchanges of words he left, with me thinking what he might have said, had I not been so alert!

One night we had an air raid, with a few stray planes dropping their bombs before flying out to sea. Our platoon took bicycles and went out to investigate. We found that a row of bombs had fallen close to the church with one scoring a direct hit on our cookhouse. There were a few injuries to personnel and the quartermaster's store was caught. We had more and better food for a while because the quartermaster received more rations to replace damaged stocks. This was about all the excitement we had at this very quiet, lonely village. It was winter so there was little to do at night when there was no guard duty. Whenever possible I entertained the lads in our billet with my mouth organ or harmonica.

Soon we were on the move again, this time to Scotland[2]. It was a very severe winter when we moved and after much speculation as to where we would be going, there was a lot of hard work to be done packing for the move. At the end of a long tiring journey, we found ourselves coming to a halt at a large tweed mill in Galashiels. The army had taken the mill over for the duration of the war.

After settling in, the strict training intensified, with many route marches and manoeuvres at night and in the daytime with the rest of the brigade. One scheme lasted three days and nights. In this we covered over eighty miles against imaginary opposition. The weather was very cold, especially at night, as we had to try to get a few hours sleep wherever we happened to be out in the country. On the third day out, two other lads and I chased a rabbit, caught and killed it. We put it on the platoon truck and took it back to barracks. One of the cooks at the cookhouse did us a favour and made a rabbit pie for us. Just before evening meal we collected the pie, and then the evening meal. Feeling quite hungry after being out in the open air for three days, one lad and I ate the lot between us. The other lad didn't fancy the challenge, but we enjoyed ours, which gave us a very full stomach, but no after effects.

During the time we were at Galashiels a *Garrison Theatre* was organised for anyone wanting to contribute to the show. I was asked by the sergeant to play my harmonica. The show was at the local theatre which housed about a thousand. Without much preparation I selected a few nice tunes and gave the pianist the titles of the selection. With no rehearsal he followed me beautifully, which ended

---

2   1st January 1941

with good applause. The whole show was a complete success, and the local population took us into their hearts. We were invited back to their homes where they made us welcome.

All rather too quickly came the news that we would be going abroad. We were given embarkation leave quite hurriedly. The journey home was bad enough but worse was to come.

While we were on leave, heavy falls of snow with cold winds caused drifting and freezing conditions. It made the journey back to Galashiels very difficult. Starting back in good time, so we thought, we made progress to Birmingham without much trouble. There we found lots of soldiers stranded on the platforms. The trains to Scotland were six hours late. Many of our lads were waiting. In the early hours of the morning we reported to the Railway Transport Officer (R.T.O.) to get our passes signed as proof of being unable to proceed on the journey.

When the train finally did come, it was with slow progress, and great difficulty on the long travel north, through drifts of snow, in the early hours of the morning.

By the time we arrived back in barracks to check in at the guard-room, we were sixteen hours late. We were immediately put on a charge, to appear before the Commanding Officer. One by one the charges were read out. Then I was asked, "What do you have to say?"

I told my story and showed my pass signed by the R.T.O. Neither the weather conditions nor the signed pass made any difference: this was the army. We all got seven days *C.B.*, in other words: confined to barracks with extra fatigues.

Next day I had a temperature, so I reported sick. The medical officer sent me immediately to the local hospital. I was kept in for a week with 'flu and nursed by civilian nurses which was great. By remaining there for a week I avoided doing my *C.B.*, which was a relief.

Our move overseas failed to materialise, but instead we moved to the Midlands, close to home at Nuneaton. This gave us a better chance of getting back home.[3]

During the summer of 1941 we were sleeping six to a tent in the grounds of Arbury Park. While I was on leave for the weekend, the terrific air-raid on Coventry took place, which is close to Arbury. Lots of shrapnel fell in the grounds and quite close to the tents. Fortunately not many were injured. Being on leave, we didn't know exactly where the raid had been, but we heard it and knew that it was a very heavy raid over several hours.

Also during the summer the Battalion put on a spectacular tattoo display, in which I took part. The training for the event was very hard, but very rewarding. Ours was a drilling display without a word of command. Free admission was given to many hundreds of the local people, who enjoyed a spectacular event to brighten up the weary, hard-working days of the war.[4] We were welcomed everywhere around Arbury and Nuneaton after that.

It was while I was at Arbury that I started smoking. At the time we were rationed with cigarettes and chocolate. I swapped my ration of cig's for a chocolate ration, with each one in turn in my tent. Before long, one disgruntled customer thought I had missed his share of cigarette ration out, and believed a closer friend had been favoured. My next ration of cigarettes was issued just before my appointment to the dentist. On that day while I waited in the dentist's, I felt the cigarettes in my pocket and decided to smoke them myself. This, I thought, would end the unpleasant accusations. I continued to smoke my ration after that, but I missed my extra chocolate. It was not until 1946 that I gave up the smoking habit.

Just when we were settling in nicely at Arbury we heard that we were to move. "But where to now?" we asked ourselves. Luckily it was still in the Midlands: to Cannock. More packing and unpacking for us to do!

The company was billeted in Cannock town which was good for us when we wanted to go out. The other companies of the Battalion

---

3   The move south took place on 5th April 1941.
4   The Tattoo was held on 31st August before an audience of 15,000. £500 was raised to endow a *Cambridgeshire* cot in the Nuneaton hospital.

were in surrounding places, one being at Rugeley. They did a lot of training on Cannock Chase.

At weekends, unless we were on duty, the lads living in the Birmingham area went on unofficial leave. Sometimes on Sundays a church parade was called. One weekend I went home when a parade was unexpectedly called. On roll call I was one of the absentees. I was on a charge. With no excuses I was on seven days *C.B.* Fortunately for me again, I was sent to Rugeley to another company the next day, for a week or more. For a second time I escaped doing my *C.B.* This made me wiser before the event in future.

My work at Rugeley involved making grease traps, and fly-proof preparation surrounds for the cookhouse. I enjoyed that work very much, because no-one bothered me and it was good training for what was to come. When I had met their requirements I was taken back to Cannock.

I remember buying a French top pocket watch at Cannock. It was a nice watch with a decorative face which I liked. The watch worked well, but it lost time, so I took it back to the shop. Before I was able to get my watch back we were on the move again. Many years later when I returned after the war, I went back to Cannock. I still remembered the watch, but I dare-say the shopkeeper had forgotten.

Rumours of a move prior to going overseas persisted, and everybody seemed to be eager to get into the action instead of moving around to new training grounds.

The next move was to Lichfield Barracks[5]. We trained there for embarkation, checking stores and equipment, packing and unpacking, to see how quickly we could do it. We knew there would be no false alarm this time when we were issued with tropical kit. Furthermore, we knew our destination would probably be the Middle East, not Europe. During embarkation leave, Mary and I agreed to get engaged. There were emotional farewells as I left loved ones for the unknown future.

---

5   A Regimental history named the location as Whittington Barracks, Lichfield.

Embarkation

It was October 1941 when the Battalion moved from Lichfield to Liverpool by train[6], where we boarded the *S.S.Orcades*. We were part of the 18th Division, about to do our bit for the war effort. Escorted out to sea by warships[7], our convoy zigzagged our way across the Atlantic in mountainous seas. After several days out we were met by American warships[8], including an aircraft carrier. Our small escort, by comparison to our American one, left us, as we continued in icy Arctic seas for a few more days. We docked in Halifax (Canada)[9] and changed ships. This ship was the luxurious American ship *U.S.S. West Point*, which we were told was built to gain the *Blue Ribbon*. It was formerly named *U.S.S. America*.[10]

We sailed south[11], passing the time keeping fit, playing bingo, or watching films. Soon we put into Trinidad for two days[12]. Continuing south in glorious sunshine we approached the Equator. A ducking chair was fixed at the edge of the swimming pool on top deck.

---

6 27th October 1941
7 Departed 28th October, rendezvous with remainder of fleet (from Clyde) on 30th October.. The convoy was designated *Outward North 30* and included the vessels: *Orcades, Oronsay, Andes, Sobiesky, Duchess of Atholl, Rena Del Pacifico, Warwick Castle* and *Durban Castle*.
8 2nd November
9 8th November
10 The *USS West Point* was part of a convoy was named *William Sail 12X* which consisted of:
   Aircraft Carrier *Ranger*; Heavy Cruiser *Quincey*; Heavy Cruiser *Vincennes*; Troopship *Mount Vernon 1*; Troopship *Leonard Wood*; Troopship *Joseph T Dickman*; Troopship *Orizaba*; Troopship *Wakefield*; Troopship *West Poin*t; Fleet Oiler *Cimarron*; Destroyer *Wainwright*; Destroyer *Moffe*tt; Destroyer *McDougal*; Destroyer *Winslow*; Destroyer *Mayrant*; Destroyer *Rhind*; Destroyer *Rowan*; Destroyer *Trippe* .
11 Departed 10th November
12 Commencing 17th November

Sailors dressed up as King Neptune and his courtiers, who rounded up officers, or men, to celebrate crossing the line. As we crossed the line, victims were tried and ducked in the pool; hosepipes were used on everyone within range. It was a spectacular, unforgettable experience for which we were given a certificate; this certificate remains a most treasured possession.

Ancient Order of the Deep

TO all sailors wherever ye may be, and to all living things of the Sea, GREETING: Know ye that on November 24, 1941 in Lat. 0° and Long. 40° 28′ W.

Serving on the U. S. S. WEST POINT bound south for Capetown, Union of South Africa, was found worthy to be a TRUSTY SHELLBACK, and was initiated into the Solemn Mysteries of the Ancient Order of the Deep.

Davy Jones
His Majesty's Scribe

Neptunus Rex
Ruler of the Raging Main

Continuing to sail south our next port of call was Cape Town[13]. It was announced that we could have shore leave, to our great delight: half of the ship's company one day and half the next. Dressed in tropical kit (shorts and shirt with topee) we were met by the local people, who invited twos or threes out with them. I, with a few others, was taken by car for a tour of their lovely town. One public building we were taken to gave me the surprise of my life; I had never seen anything quite like it. While it was brilliant sunshine outside, we entered inside, and looked up to the quite high ceiling. It looked as if the day had suddenly changed to night. The starry night effect ceiling was so real; it looked as if there was no roof to the building. We were

---

13 Arrived 9th December. Troops were made aware of USA's entry into the war following the Japanese attack on Pearl Harbour.

then taken back to the family home, situated close to, and with a view of Table Mountain. It was a lovely house, with a garden and fruit trees that were laden with peaches, bananas and oranges. The people were so hospitable. We were taken back to the ship, expressing our gratitude. The next day we stayed on board while the other half had shore leave. Then the following day it all happened again. A ladies' marching band came past, playing especially for us. The next day[14] we set sail again, around the Cape northwards.

Christmas Day was spent at sea, with all the trimmings, but thoughts turned first to home, then to our uncertain future. We were going to war; we knew that, but where? The convoy sailed on, life aboard was relaxed, away from the threat of U-Boats. I had the almost daily job of taking the platoon, and anyone who cared to join in, on physical training.

As the huge ship sailed northwards in the Indian Ocean, the weather was beautiful and sunny every day. On deck, looking out to sea, it was interesting to see the acrobatic dolphins following us for long periods. Now and again we saw flying fish leaping and flying above the water. They seemed to be putting on a display for our benefit as a thank you for dumping our waste food overboard. The American cooks fed us very well but they threw away food in waste. We were told that if food had been brought up from the hold to be prepared and it wasn't on the menu that day, it was dumped.

We now expected to make port on the North-East coast of Africa to reinforce the Middle-East troops. But, as the days went by, that rumour faded. At last we came into land, to discover the port of call was Bombay, India. So we had crossed the Equator a second time, but without another ceremony. It was now eleven weeks, at least, since we had left Liverpool.

Then to our delight we began to disembark[15]. We were marched to the railway station. The poverty and squalor was astonishing, after the luxury of Cape Town. The 18th Division, of which we were a part, called at other ports on the East African coast. Our Battalion

14 Departed 13th December
15 Arrived in Bombay on 27th December but did not disembark until 29th.

moved by train to Ahmednager, some distance inland from Bombay. We arrived to find a large camp with numerous huts, all well spaced out. Our hut was forty to fifty yards away from the cookhouse, and as we were to discover, it was a dangerous walk. We collected our meals in our mess tins, gingerly holding the contents out before us, but before getting too far, one of many kite hawks swooped down from behind. With such a swift, graceful glide just missing the topee (head cover) they would snatch the choicest part of your meal. It was no good going back for more. Luckily, we could buy cakes and other snacks from the Indian camp vendors. The tea sold by them was, I think, the nicest mug of tea I've ever tasted.

The serious business of training hard continued here for another two weeks and then we were told we were going to move again. It had been hard thirsty work, to train in extremely hot sunshine, and, with the daily attacks from the Kite Hawks, we were glad to know that we were leaving. Our mystery move took us back to Bombay where we found that we were boarding the same ship again. On 19th January we were sailing away from Bombay, due south, linking up with the rest of the convoy. When we had changed course in an easterly direction, after several days afloat, our destination was revealed. We were given lectures on the formidable defences of Singapore, and the inefficiency of the Japanese forces. On the twenty-eighth of January 1942 we saw land, and with it a Japanese spotter plane, later to be followed by a squadron of fighting planes which began to attack the convoy. As we took cover below decks the ship picked up speed and vibrated as if it had run aground. We had survived the attack, but other ships were not so fortunate. The speed, for which the ship was built, had helped us to reach Singapore ahead of all the convoy.

The Battle for Singapore

It was a speedy but well organised disembarkation, but as we walked down one gangplank, the R.A.F. personnel were going up another to board the ship.[16] They were leaving, and so were the last few Hurricanes which flew overhead. As we marched away, sniper fire was heard quite close by. We were hurried to the suburbs of the city, but nowhere did we find any kind of defence in this so called fortress. Evidence showed that people had left their houses in a hurry. It was difficult to realize why we had gone to the other side of the world to this small island of Singapore, but our job was to act out orders and not to reason why!

Formations of bombers were systematically destroying the docks, warehouses and the city itself. We learnt that the ship which followed ours, the *Empress of Asia,* was bombed and sunk in the harbour. Lots of equipment was lost. Our first few days were spent among rubber trees, to adjust ourselves to whatever was to come[17]. My sergeant detailed me to erect a screen for a latrine, and naturally I asked him what I had to use to do the job. His answer came back quickly: "Use your ingenuity." So I began to scrounge, unaccustomed as I was, to collect material for the temporary screen. The job was done, with a little ingenuity!

---

16 The Battalion War Diary reported that upon arrival at Singapore they were met by senior officers of the 18th Division who told them that they were too late. Malaya was lost, Singapore was next and there was no escape. The Battalion CO, Lieutenant Colonel Gerald Goodwin Carpenter advised his officers not to tell the men.

17 The Battalion spent a couple of days billeted in Joo Chiat Police Station, Katong, on the outskirts of Singapore City.

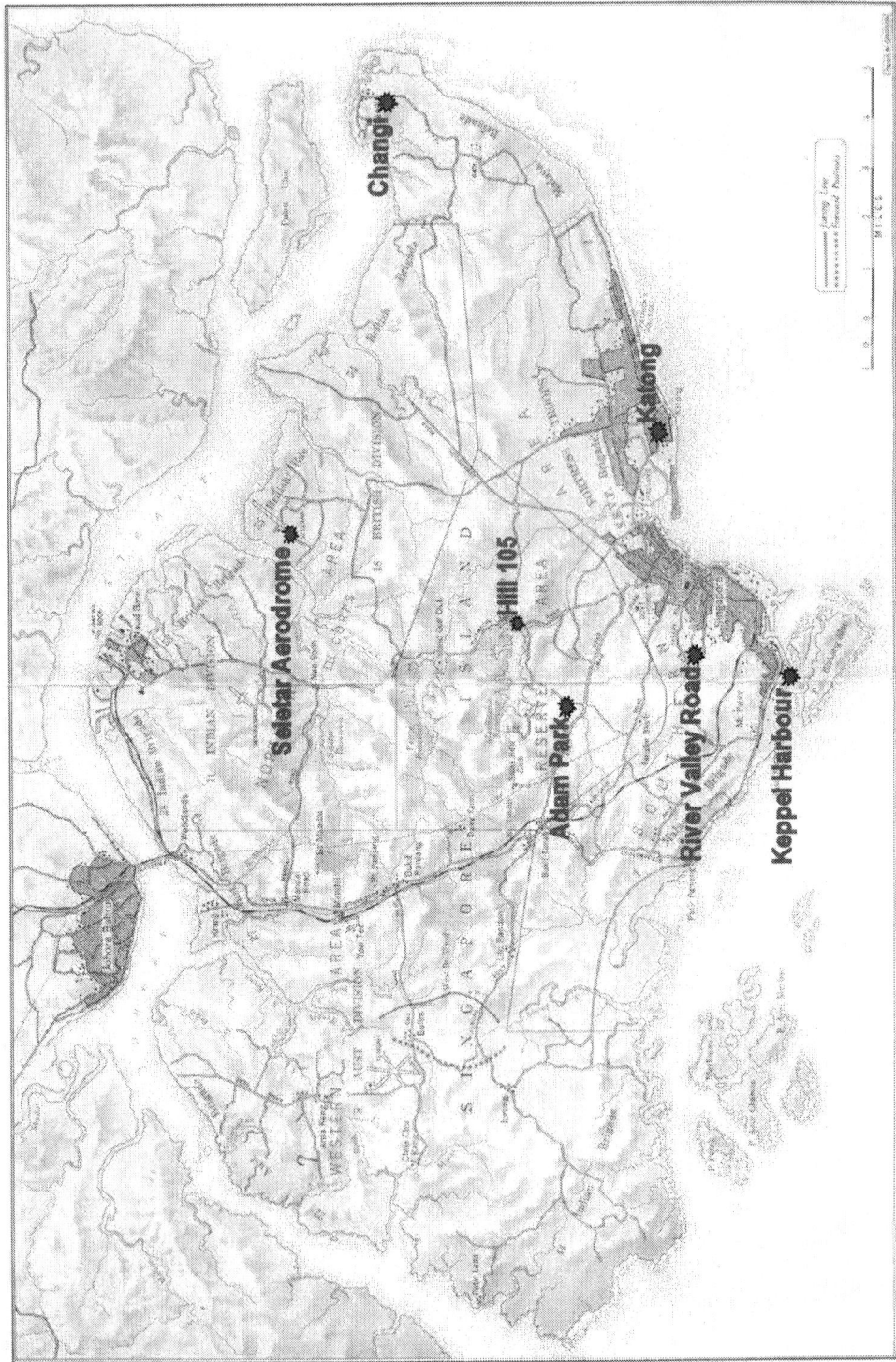

Changi

Katong

Seletar Aerodrome

Hill 105

Adam Park

River Valley Road

Keppel Harbour

We were moved again soon after to a defensive location near to the causeway, which linked the island with the mainland[18]. By then the Japanese forces had leap-frogged down the coast of Malaya, infiltrating and overrunning the combined British, Australian, Indian and other forces. With no air protection they had to retreat. They came back over the causeway, shells screaming over them and us, dropping not far away. Our own guns opened up with deafening reports from close behind. It was too close for comfort. We didn't sleep night or day for many days. Then the inevitable happened. The Royal Engineers blew up the causeway and terrific explosions ensued. The night sky was illuminated with flashes from all directions. In the daytime the bombers picked off the guns one by one.[19] Quite soon afterwards we were told that the Japs had landed in large numbers on the north-west coast. We were ordered to take up positions near Bukit Tima.[20]

The platoon dug in once more in the front lawn of a large house, which was situated on a hill. The Battalion H.Q. took cover under or around the house. The Companies A, B, C and D moved closer to the enemy. Fierce fighting took place when the Japs brought up tanks. Our forces didn't have any. We could see soldiers running, several yards to our left, and then we heard screams as one of our Companies had set alight the wooded area where the enemy were. A few of our platoon were sent out to join the Companies. We heard that they'd been killed. I was sent out with a few others, to take ammunition to our lads. It was a perilous journey, because a spotter plane overhead was machine-gunning us. A concrete monsoon drainpipe was our

---

18 On 1st February the Battalion moved to Seletar Aerodrome on the north coast of the island. The Battalion War Diary states "from the commencement of the invasion, until the units were ordered to leave Seletar Aerodrome, we were completely in the dark as to the state of operations."

19 On 8th February the Battalion moved to a forward position at the aerodrome, repacing the Kapurtala Infantry Battalion whose morale was described as 'at nil' in the Battalion War Diary.

20 On 11th February, the Battalion moved south and took up a position at Hill 105, just south-east of Macritchie Reservoir. The following day they moved further south to the area of Adam Park, HQ Company initially occupying the RASC camp immediately to the east of Adam Road.

saviour. We crawled into this with the ammunition and no-one was hit. We delivered the ammunition safely then made a safe return to base. At this stage, the battalion had put up stiff resistance and held positions, but the Japs had closed three sides. Our platoon was ordered to take a position on a hill.

We moved forward towards the new position to occupy what looked like a Chinese burial ground[21]. We crawled to position ourselves along the top of the ridge. On the other side of the ridge the Japanese had moved within mortar range of us. Their observation planes flew above, machine-gunning us as we lay waiting for the attack. They must have given our position to their mortars, because a terrific bombardment began. They had our range perfectly. Mortar bombs fell amongst us, one whistled just over my head and dropped on the other side of the grave where I lay. It fizzed and popped! I thought "This one is for me." But fortunately it was a dud. We were pinned down; waiting for the attack, but it never came. Thankfully there was a lull. The word came for us to move to our original position at the base of the hill, near B.H.Q.[22]

In this position the long range shells whistled overhead with menacing intensity. We had dug in facing the main road, at the corner of Adam Road and Bukit Tima Road[23]. We were to help defend B.H.Q. at all costs. Our water truck was hit by a shell and the driver was killed. Japanese snipers tied themselves to the tops of trees and picked off our men, killing and wounding several. They were tied so that they didn't drop when our soldiers fired at them, so that we had no knowledge of success. Our mortar platoon had laid down a heavy barrage against the advancing Japanese tanks, destroying some, but

---

21 This incident probably took place on 13th February.

22 B.H.Q. was housed in No. 7, Adam Park. The Battalion War Diary, 14th February: "One very satisfactory feature of the days fighting was the quantity of beer, all ranks were able to consume … while the evening action was on progress nearly every weapon pit had one bottle at alert, so to speak, and one in reserve."

23 On the 15th February, Jack was dug in on the eastern edge of Adam Park, in front of No. 8, facing the junction of Adam Road and what is now known as Arcadia Road.

we had no tanks at all, nor 'planes, to give us a chance to hold up the Japanese on all sides.

We were told that the commanding officer was preparing to break through the enemy lines at all costs. It came as a great surprise, later, to hear the news that we were to lay down arms. The ceasefire was agreed and the capitulation of all troops to the Japanese forces was to take effect from four-thirty on this day, the fifteenth of February[24].

We were tired out, mentally and physically, with no sleep for many days at a time, and very little food in the last few days. Now we had to wait, for what? We had no idea. The only thing we knew was that we had to wait where we were, fearful of what might happen to us. One of our sergeants was heard to say, "Why did the Good Lord let me come to this, and leave my wife and children?" as he shed some tears.

We had trained for two years before embarkation, but not for the kind of action which was forced upon us. The Japs had come down from the north to the south of Malaya by way of a well prepared method of infiltrating agents. They knew where to strike, and strike hard. With the help of unhindered navy and air force, the same method quickly rolled back some of the best units in the British Army, right to Singapore. On the island of Singapore there was nowhere to hide or to retreat to. We were trapped, civilians and soldiers. Those who did try to get away by boat were either machine-gunned or sunk by the Jap navy or air-force.

We waited in silence, looking in front and left to right wondering where the enemy would come from, as we had a good field of view. If they came from the direction we were looking we would see them approach. Our rifles, ammunition, grenades and equipment were laid out in front of the trench. Apart from the lads in our platoon, we

---

24 The order to cease fire was communicated to the Battalion at 3.30pm, to take effect at 4pm. War Diary: "It proved rather difficult to shout the instructions across the road to "A" Coy. but by 1630 hours all sounds of firing on the Bn front had died down." Around 5.00 a Bren gun fired upon Japanese troops collecting their wounded and in retaliation their tanks and small arms opened up on No.17 Adam Park which housed the Cambridgeshire's Regimental Aid Post (RAP), setting it alight.

couldn't see anyone.

Quite suddenly, at the back of us, appeared a Jap officer with one of ours, and a few equally small Japanese soldiers, heavily laden with equipment and camouflage. For a moment it was quite frightening as they stood above us shouting orders or something that we couldn't understand. Then in English we heard "All men come. Hurry, hurry." We got out of the trench and followed to the front of the house on the hill. We only had our tropical kit on, and our haversack with a few personal things in. We were searched and many watches, pens or valuable items were taken away. Then we were led to the tennis court on the other side of the hill below the house. The house had been our B.H.Q. and was now occupied by the Japs.[25]

There were about five hundred Cambridgeshires and a few Suffolks squeezed into the tennis court. A Jap machine gun was manned at each corner outside the wire netting, pointing menacingly inwards. We were locked in and at the mercy of our captors and we feared the worst. There were no toilets provided, which made conditions worse, and no food given. It was getting dark and cold then, so we just huddled together trying to rest until next morning.

The next day the worst wounded were permitted to receive attention nearby, some of whom were badly burnt when their post was set on fire. Our officers were taken away, leaving us with sergeant-major's rank and below. They had the immediate task of clearing one corner of the area for latrines. This they were able to do with willing hands, and very few tools. Even so, it soon became intolerably smelly,

---

25 War Diary: "At 1730 hours the Commanding Officer and Adjt went down to Adam Rd to meet the Japanese. ... As a note in the Adjt's pocket diary states, 'Bn taken prisoner – but taken in their original positions. The unit was not defeated and did not retire.'"

The Diary, written by Lt Col Carpenter, concluded: "The unit did not receive any intelligence from the rear, and for the greater part of the action were completely in the dark as to happenings, other than those on our immediate front.

"Singapore fell owing to the lack of plans, orders and power of command.

"Whenever we had the chance the British, Australian and Indian Soldier proved himself immeasurably superior to the Japanese, who are nothing more than an overrated crowd of gangsters."

getting worse as the sun rose high above. Those who were nearest to it came off worse, and I wasn't far away. During the day a few at a time were let out escorted, to get water, but it wasn't clean tap water. We'd had little chance of a wash at all since we'd landed on the island; in fact we hadn't had our shoes off all that while. We were treated like animals penned in a cage, when the Japs threw some hard army biscuits and ration chocolate over the netting. We had to suffer this treatment for five days before we were taken out of those cramped, stinking conditions. I was glad and thankful that I had survived the fighting without being wounded.

It was a great relief when we were herded out of the tennis court to line up and move off. The sick and wounded that could walk were in front, followed by the more severely wounded, aided or carried by any method. The rest followed behind and took turns to help. Along the roadsides as we walked, we passed dead bodies of soldiers and civilians, still lying in the position where they had been shot or burned to death with flame throwers. We passed by a public building surrounded with a cast iron spiked railing. On the spikes were the heads of a number of Chinese, with blood dripping. They were more than likely executed and put on display for us to see. There were Japanese flags everywhere on buildings as we staggered on away from the city. The Japanese troops were celebrating their victory.

Our celebrations were over for longer than we realized. The sun was hot again and we were very tired. Thankfully we were given a rest in the shade of some trees. As we rested, some of our army trucks came up with British and Australian drivers. Our medical officer asked the Jap in charge to allow the severely wounded to ride. The drivers told us that everyone was now at Changi, and that was where we were going. It seemed as if we had been the last to be captured, or kept to suffer longer. The wounded got the ride to Changi, the rest of us had to walk, which was a few more miles on. While we were on that walk, we got a taste of the way life as a prisoner of the Japs was going to be. They had no respect for the sick or lame. Anyone who lagged behind was prodded with any weapon or slapped. If anyone failed to act on a command they were slapped, even though not a word of Japanese was understood. The first words we understood were "O.K. car", American slang plus "car", which they used after many question words. The other word was "*dami-dami*" which was a scolding word for "no good."

In and Out of Changi

Eventually we reached Changi prison camp, worn out, tired and starving. The camp was packed by the time our company had arrived, so we had to settle for anything we could find. A meal of rice and watery soup was ready for us quite quickly as the cooks had been informed of our imminent arrival by the truck drivers who had stopped to pick up the wounded. Our cooks, being away from the front line, were taken to Changi after capitulation. After our meal and a drink of tea without milk or sugar, we felt better. Next we managed to get a wash and clean up, before retiring to our hut for a well earned rest. Needless to say we slept that night whatever the discomfort was, sleeping on bamboo slats.

It was a great relief to be able to relax the next day with regular meals, even if it was mainly rice. The Japs didn't bother us for a while. They placed the responsibility on our own junior officers, who were then with us, for good order and discipline. It was back to the parade ground again.

Each morning and evening we were lined up for roll-call. Instead of forming in threes, as we did in the British army, we now had to form fives as did the Japanese army, probably because they couldn't count in threes. This didn't make it any easier for the Japs to count us. Often we had to wait for several recounts before we were dismissed. After roll call and breakfast of rice and sugar, our own NCOs detailed us for jobs of administration in our area. There were lots of things to do to improve our way of living, especially in the Singapore climate with flies about. When the daily jobs were finished there was time to wander around the camp to find out who had survived. The wounded and the worst of the sick personnel were in the adjoining Roberts Hospital, but this was grossly overcrowded. The minor injured or sick could attend sick parade, to receive whatever treatments were available. The change in diet affected many men, some with sores, some with upset stomachs, and some soon showed signs of vitamin deficiency. The result was a great struggle for survival and some couldn't make it. The cemetery started at Changi, soon enlarged with three or four funerals a day.

It was at Changi where we saw huge pill boxes and guns pointing out to sea. They were the only defences installed to stop the invader. Naturally, as they pointed out to sea in a fixed position, they never fired a shot in anger. The Japs came from the opposite direction. It was at Changi too, that I first saw coconut trees, but they were soon stripped and restricted by, and for, the Japs. Occasionally in the evenings, when we were more organised, someone would give a lecture, or we would have a debate. One such lecture I remember was "Should sex be taught in schools?" This, I think, was the forerunner of a never ending debate. Permission was given to make a stage and put on shows, and very soon the talented ones among us were able to form a good concert party. Musicians found instruments, or made them, to provide the accompanying music. The result was a top class show which relieved the boredom for a while. Rumours of the progress of the war spread around at these gatherings, but at that stage it was not very cheery.

It was at Changi, three weeks after Singapore surrendered that I had my first birthday in captivity. Who would have thought that my birthday treat was little more than a helping of boiled rice? In fact the day was just another boring, depressing day with only one thought: "How long were we to be kept prisoners of war, and could we, by some miracle, be freed to get out of this miserable experience?" The prophets in the camp gave us high hopes at times, but each prediction came to nothing. After dark, lying on bamboo slats, trying to get some rest was difficult enough, but with the torment of mosquitoes, lice and the croaking bullfrogs it was worse. Little did we know then that things were going to get much worse.

After many weeks we heard that some of us would be moving. Groups of one hundred or so were selected with intervals in between each group. We heard that they were going to Singapore to clean up.

Our turn came sometime in May, I think. We were to march to Singapore, a distance of some twenty miles. The fittest were selected, so this time we didn't have to support the sick. Our shoes were getting a bit worn now, but we made it, tired, exhausted, gasping for a drink and hungry. After walking for several hours we arrived at the camp called *River Valley Road Camp.* Lining up in fives for the inevitable roll-call, we waited for ages while we were counted several times to assure the new guards that no-one had escaped. Then a further wait while the officers in charge were given orders, and we were allotted our space in a hut.

The huts were about one hundred metres long by six metres wide, with a two metre gangway between two-tier platforms, all constructed with bamboo. The roof was formed with atap leaves folded over a cane to make a strip a few feet long. These were laid in tile fashion to overlap. The only thing to say in favour of them was that in daytime they provided shade, as we were to find out, but when it rained it was not very waterproof. My bed space was on the top tier, gained by straight bamboo ladders every four or five metres apart.

Very soon after settling in, the sound of mess tins heralded the arrival of a meal. It was usual to queue at the end of each hut for a ladle of rice, a smaller one of *vegetable water* with maybe a floating piece of meat, and a mug of slightly sweetened tea with no milk. This was the main meal. The morning breakfast of rice and a teaspoon of sugar was at the break of day, to prepare us for roll-call at eight-thirty. After roll call we were marched off to work. We worked until about five, with an hour's break approximately, then marched back, had a wash, a meal and then roll-call again at about seven in the evening. For this the Japs paid the privates ten cents a day, so every ten days we received a dollar. This enabled us to buy a few eggs or bananas.

The camp had a dirty looking stream on the one side, which was a breeding ground for mosquitoes. On the opposite side was the road after which the camp was named. Facing us on that road was a big Chinese house with a balcony. They would sit there watching us, but the Jap guards had eyes on them too, in case any messages were passed.

The Japs now decided that we should learn some basic Japanese, so on roll-call we had to call out their equivalent to our numbers which

39

went: *Itchi, Nee, San, See, Go, Rocko, Sitchi, Hatchi, Cou, Jou.* Our own sergeant major would quickly count beforehand, and would tell the last man what to shout. So long as the first row counted correctly, the numbers counted after *Jou*, for ten, the remainder shouted "Jack, Queen, King, Ace" or anything, as long as the last man shouted correctly as informed. We thought it was highly amusing, and the Japs seemed satisfied. The equivalent for attention, number, salute to the right, and left, stand at ease, or rest, followed. As we marched to work, which was about one and a half miles away, we were now able to salute Jap officers along the road, at the order shouted by the proud Japanese sergeant in charge. Some of the salutes were not very complimentary!

We were separated into working parties according to the trades or jobs we could do. The cooks in normal army life stayed in camp to prepare meals, often working in very poor conditions, with little equipment, and not much to cook but rice. They tried to do their best, I am sure, but the cry often went up: "Change the cooks!" The cooks were changed often, but the result was very much the same. However, a scheme was arranged for deductions from pay to buy extras to make the food more tasty and satisfying. The extras though were only enough to make any difference to one meal a day, so we were always hungry.

I was selected into the group of workers for carpenters and other building workers. Our first job was to construct timber frames to form the sides for several warehouses and then roof trusses and erect them. Then finally we put on the roof purlins for others to finish off. This was quite a long job and on a good site. The Jap engineers worked with us, but it was difficult for us to understand sometimes, what was required of us. We soon learned when we had gone wrong when they shouted "*Dami Dami*", meaning 'No good', followed by swear words "*Canaro, Buggaro.*" Many times we saw somebody being hit with whatever was at hand. The punishment very often went too far for lack of understanding. I remember a particular prisoner made to hold a heavy piece of wood above his head with both arms stretched. As he lowered his arms, when he couldn't hold it any longer, he was hit hard on his arms, back, or face. After a while, our own officer in charge tried to make a protest to the two Jap privates who seemed to be enjoying the suffering. They promptly took the piece of heavy wood off the prisoner and made the officer do the same. Rank meant nothing as far as prisoners were concerned to the Japs. Sometimes as we marched to work along the tree-lined road, we would see Chinese men or women tied with their hands behind the trees. The words in English above their heads said "Robber", "Thief" or other crimes committed. This was plainly for us to take notice. It was quite a relief to get back to camp each day, from the fear of the unpredictable, mad fits of temper of which some guards were capable.

After work and evening meal, a well earned rest, and evening Roll-call (*Tenko*), we occupied our spare time in many ways. A few of my platoon were together in the hut and we played card games together. A few of us passed the time away drawing, either freehand or technical. With the help of a twelve inch ruler which I had acquired, I drew a plan of a bungalow which I thought might be the house of my dreams in the unpredictable future. It was drawn to scale on a piece of paper from an exercise book. This took many hours to do, a most interesting pastime, and I was fortunate to preserve it and bring it home on release. Other pastimes arranged for evenings were lectures and educational classes. I attended lectures and a maths class. Language classes were very popular. Up to now our morale was high, though the food was poor and the work hard. Every tenth working day we had a day in camp. Everyone was busy with the task of washing clothes, a blanket or whatever we were fortunate enough to keep. Then the main task of the day was to take off the bamboo slats, which was infected with bugs and lice, from your bed space. A fire was made close to the hut where everyone passed the slats through the flames to eliminate the pests. A better night's sleep was had the following night.

The poor food and conditions were the main reason for many skin complaints, made much worse by the irritating bugs and lice. I developed ringworms on my legs and backside. When I couldn't stand the irritation any longer I reported to the medical officer. Medical supplies were very limited, so alternative measures were tried. My ringworms were dabbed with a liquid which tingled and burnt so badly that I ran all around the hut before I stopped. I learned afterwards that it was battery acid, but I was glad to have some treatment to check the ringworm, and it actually worked.

Our first chance to send a message home came while we were at this camp, almost six months after being a prisoner of war. It was a printed card and very brief, with space for a name only for us to put on. It read: "I am well / I am ill / I am in hospital.- Please see that .... is taken care." This was a waste of time anyway, because none were received back home to my knowledge. There seemed to be no point in thinking about home at this stage. We were prisoners of war, and the war didn't seem to be going in our favour. The news we did get gave us very little hope of being freed at all. I remember thinking that the only thing to do was to forget home altogether, and accept the fact that where we were was our life and home. This, I think, helped me to survive, because everything seemed much better than it actually was, even the food seemed more satisfying.

The daily routine changed very little, except that more men were sick with malaria, dysentery, and malnutrition. Consequently the workforce was smaller, but the tasks set each day were greater. The weather in Singapore, incidentally, is more or less the same the whole year, with daytime temperatures in the nineties. At any time in the day though, falling out of the clouds which minutes ago were not there, a heavy torrent of rain would come, followed by a fine rainbow. In the space of a few minutes, the blue skies would return with the hot sun, making steam rise up to form a sticky heat. This would be tolerable in normal conditions, but it didn't make good working conditions for us. Tempers frayed on both sides, but as underdogs we were at the mercy of the Jap guards, who took delight in showing each other how to punish anyone, on the slightest excuse. I must say, I was lucky up to this point.

After the warehouses were finished, I was put in a party to build a bridge over the river which ran close by. The first job was to get quite long and heavy steel girders from one side to the other, to rest on bases formed in concrete. With no crane or any other mechanical aid, we thought the Japs must be mad, but they had other ideas. We were the substitute for cranes. With a lot of shouting in a language we couldn't understand, the girders were moved by pushing on rollers on the ground. The first one moved at right angles to the river with one end up to the nearside bank. The second one moved slowly on rollers in direct line behind it. Then the front end lifted onto a roller on the back end of the first girder. Pushing and moving rollers along the girder as they came out from behind, the second girder manoeuvred to cantilever over the first. A third girder rolled into position to follow the previous procedure. This, when positioned to cantilever the second girder, and far enough to span the river, was pushed off to drop close to its final position. When one was over, the same procedure followed and gradually the bridge took shape, but with much hard work.

We were taken one day to a place where all sorts of looted clothing was stored. Each one of us was allowed to pick up two or three items in turn. I chose a pair of swimming trunks and a blanket. These I took care of and kept until my release. Apart from the trunks, the only shirt I had was eventually ripped up for loin cloths.

In the hut were many lads from the same unit, and indeed whose homes were close to mine. It was easy to detect your own dialect amongst the rest. In our hut, in a bedspace below me, was Ronald Searle. He did a lot of drawings, and at times could be seen drawing guards' portraits, while the Japs sat innocently on the bed space opposite. After the war he was to become famous as an author and for his illustrations in books. An Australian prisoner in a nearby hut was Russell Braddon, who also went on to become an author.

With most of the clearing up and tasks in Singapore completed, the working parties were moved back to Changi. My party's turn to move back was among the first, and with mixed fortunes. We had been lucky to be moved from Changi for work in Singapore, according to the stories we heard when we got back. The Japs had demanded that all prisoners signed a declaration not to escape. Changi prisoners agreed not to sign. They were given a deadline to sign, but still refused, so they were made to march to Selarang Barracks. Built to accommodate approximately one thousand, nearly eighteen times that number were crammed in, on meagre rations and no sanitary arrangements. The stories we heard of this were horrible, and many did not survive. They had no alternative but to sign when the Japs threatened to move the sick and dying into the camp as well. Our officers had heard of this at River Valley Camp so we were recommended to sign.

The food back at Changi seemed worse than before and resulted in many skin complaints. In fact, I think everyone suffered from at least one skin disorder as a result of bad diet and lack of basic essentials. There were more deaths, occurring unnecessarily through lack of medicines. Operations were performed in primitive ways, but with outstanding skill, by the medical officers.

44

It was about this time, some eight months after surrender that we heard the news of Red Cross parcels being brought into camp. The one rumour we were longing to be true materialized when we were each issued with a few tins of fruit, corned beef, milk and cigarettes. The bulk of the Red Cross food was given in to the cookhouse to improve meals, which it undoubtedly did. My share was very carefully kept until later and rationed out and enjoyed as a real luxury. I was also lucky to be selected to be in need of a new pair of boots and a bush hat, as supplies were limited. These I also guarded with great care. We were very grateful for this South African Red Cross supply, which also included medicines for the doctors and surgeons.

The news and rumours at this time were not good at all, but our officers in charge insisted on army discipline. It seemed so useless to drill and salute as before, when we were all prisoners. Without it though, we realised life would have been much worse. Good hygiene, where possible, was insisted upon, and regular inspections of huts, cookhouses, and latrines took place. There was some thieving of other's possessions, which was soon dealt with. Little did we realize it was to help us in the three years to follow to keep our self respect and hope for a chance to survive.

Travelling North

Just as we were settling down again in Changi, it was announced that working parties were to be formed with the fittest of us to work on a railway somewhere up north. A party of over 600 Cambridgeshires was formed, some recovering from malaria and some with skin complaints. Despite this most were eager for a change, with a promise of better food and hospital care. With very little time to prepare, we were told to travel light and prepare to move. Each of us was given some rations for the day and we filled our water bottles. Then we were split into small parties to board a truck with a Jap guard to take us to Singapore railway station. We were ordered into steel-covered railway wagons, about thirty to a wagon, by Jap soldiers prodding and pushing angrily until the required number of prisoners were in each wagon. Everyone had to stand or squat in a cramped position. We were told that we would be travelling several days and nights like this, and no-one could leave the wagon at any of the stops without permission. The sliding doors were closed and so began our journey of unbearable suffering.[26]

The first day, travelling north over the causeway into Malaya, we made the best of our ordeal. The conversation was humorous with some vulgarity, but good tempers remained. It was so hot and sticky in those wagons during the day and, as we found out later, it was cold at night. To urinate was easy for those by the sliding door, but a work of art for someone in a far corner to step round and over bodies to make it to the door and back. This happened frequently as the wagons jolted and shook along to the first stop at Kuala Lumpar. The difficult part was with other calls of nature when one had to be held in a position with your backside into the outside slipstream. We were allowed off the wagons at maybe two stops a day, but there were

---

[26] A Jack departed from Changi as part of 'P' Party on 2nd November 1942. See *Appendix 6*

other stops, sometimes for fuel or water, or onto a loop line, while other trains passed. Anyone who got off at these stops for nature calls were hit with anything at hand by the Japs, but many took the risk. The local natives appeared with delicacies at most stops, but they were chased off.

With no more than two official stops each day for food, we continued to Ipoh and the Thailand border. Buckets of rice and buckets of water were placed by each wagon when we stopped for meals, but we were given just a few minutes to share it out and relieve ourselves, before everyone was ordered or prodded back into our uncomfortable cage ready to continue. The smell and the flies at these stops, caused by previous parties, made us eager to continue. The worst part of our train ride was after dusk when everyone wanted to get comfortable for the long night. With no light, except perhaps somebody's lighter flashing on now and again, elbows, knees and boots got in everyone's way. This was total humiliation, but each morning was greeted by someone cracking a joke or telling a yarn about another lad's sleeping habits. True sleep was not possible. This continued for four or five days until we reached our destination in the early hours of the morning.

With great relief and pleasure we breathed in the fresh air, glad to say goodbye to the cattle wagons we had left. Tired and very stiff, we lined up to be counted, before we were marched to the camp which was called Banpong. It was now about November 1942.[27] The promise of a good camp, good food and medical supplies was soon dashed. The camp was a filthy, muddy place, with huts constructed with bamboo and atap roofs. The roofs were leaky and the huts very frail looking. They had also been left dirty by a previous party, with flies and mosquitoes well provided for. This turned out to be a transit camp, so in a day or two we were on the move again. We heard stories from others who were already at the camp, that we were to construct a section of the railway to run from Bangkok to Moulmein in Burma.

Early in the morning, after the usual rice and watery stew, we were

---

[27] 6th November

lined up and counted and moved off to await trucks to take us to the next camp. After hours waiting in the Thailand monsoon weather, we boarded the trucks to Kanchanburi (or Kanburi for short). This was also a temporary stopping place with huts built along the same lines as in the last camp. The conditions in the camp seemed much the same as before and were as depressing as the weather.

Without much warning, we were soon on the move again. We formed up into small parties after a breakfast of rice and little else, to be marched down to the river. There we waited for small boats manned by native Thais to take us to the other side of the river. At this time of the year it was quite a fast-running, wide river, with lots of activity. The Thai natives lived on the river and sold goods of all descriptions from their boats, but we were not allowed to go near. Crossing to the other side of the river didn't take long, but it was plain to us that we were leaving civilization behind. It was the beginning of the dense, wet and sticky jungle, with lots of bamboo growing up to four or five inches in diameter and twenty feet or more high. Many different kinds of trees grew with creepers entwined.

We were marched several miles through jungle tracks to the camp which was to be our base for some time to come.[28] The camp was a muddy mess from the monsoon rains which were now in full swing. The huts followed the same crude pattern as before, each man being allotted little more than a two feet wide bamboo bed space in a continuous line each side of a hundred feet long hut. We were allowed the rest of the day off, but were told to be ready to start work the following day. This camp was known as Chungkai; quite a large camp compared with others we were to be in later. There were at least a thousand prisoners and Jap or Korean guards housed within. There were some large trees growing within the camp and a high wire fence perimeter. The camp grounds sloped down to the river bank and for once we were able to go down to wash or bathe when it was possible. There were a lot of fish in the river's muddy waters, which was waist deep a few feet out from the bank. If you didn't keep on the move, the fish bit toes and legs – especially if you had sores. The cookhouse huts were located near to the riverbank where a

---

[28] 10th November

49

lot of water was drawn for use in preparing and cooking the food.

Chungkai

As expected, at dawn the next day, after having had some rice and vegetable juice which we couldn't see to eat, we were counted and formed into small parties. We were marched off to collect picks, shovels, chunkals (a tool similar to a pick-axe but with a blade) and some wicker baskets and then we moved on to the railway embankment, passing some sections which were partly built. We halted at the section of the embankment which we were to construct. The direction and profile of this was indicated by bamboo, showing the height and rake of each side of the bank. The heights, we were to find, varied from two feet to twenty or more, according to the level of the land. Our first allotted section of embankment averaged between two to three feet. Small parties of six men worked together. Two men picked or shovelled the earth into the baskets of the other four men who carried and dumped the earth on the ground between the bamboos. This monotonous process was carried on in bad weather until the required daily task was done, which was estimated by the Jap engineers who were then in charge. We had been forewarned by our officer in charge to pace ourselves, so that our task was not finished too early in the day, otherwise the daily task would be increased. Seeing that the work was behind schedule the guards prodded and slapped men to work harder saying, "When finish, go home." These engineers were clearly pressured into getting their section of the railway done at all costs. From now on, it was punishment if the Japs were referred to as such. They were now to be referred to as *Nippon*, or a bashing ensued.

The guards must have received orders that the daily measured task had to be completed however long it took. When it became dark, some men tried to indicate the fact that it was too dark to see. They got angry answers of "*Dami dami*" and "*Buggero!*" In a short while, lamps were erected on the spot, to indicate the task had to be completed. Having failed in the effort to cut the daily task, we all worked harder to get back to camp. Exhausted, tired, wet and irritated by mosquitoes, we trudged back to our rice meal in camp - eaten in the dark - and a well earned rest. Following this, we learnt the lesson, to finish the required task at a reasonable time.

The monsoon rains continued for a while, causing flooding in the camp. The river rose so much it came up to bed-space level in many huts, and the camp became a filthy mess. Some were evacuated to higher ground. This state of things brought on illnesses such as malaria, dysentery and typhoid, to add to the agony of hard work and poor food. The night's rest was disturbed by itching and scratching caused by bugs, lice and mosquitoes. The medical officers and orderlies worked hard and skilfully in primitive conditions and a lack of proper medicine. Improvisation with tools and treatment for operations had to be admired, which no doubt saved many lives. Even so, many suffered and died who need not have done so if the Nips had been more humane and supplied medical supplies which they had in their stores.

Each day, if the required height of the embankment was only partly finished, the section being formed had to be trodden in by all men. So we strode wearily up and down until firm; thus we became human rollers. I was thankful that I had a fairly good pair of shoes then, but it was only a matter of time before they were ruined in the conditions. When a section was completed we had to start all over again, but each time it was farther away from camp. Occasionally we would have to clear anthills away, which sent ants crawling hastily around in their thousands. That was bad enough, but when a tree was disturbed which had big red ants busily at work above, they dropped onto our naked, sweating bodies and bit like hell. Each day was one big torment; no wonder some men lost the will to live when they became sick.

The work became harder as we progressed because the earth had to be taken from farther away at each side of the track. Hence the carriers had farther to walk as the day went on. Also, when the height of the track had to be more than two or three feet, it was done in layers. A day's task of two to three feet was trodden down as usual, and each following day another layer in the same way. The obvious difference was that the loads of earth had to be carried and dumped higher each day. That was never considered in the daily task by the Japs.

By the middle of December 1942, many men became victims of malaria, dysentery, beri-beri, skin disorders, tropical ulcers and typhoid. The worst cases were taken into the care of medical men in separate huts, which were no different to the other huts. The now depleted number of available fit men made it difficult to make up the required number for work parties. The Jap Commandant therefore ordered the officers out to work. At first they refused, but when threatened that they would be shot, they obeyed under protest. The Japs delighted in humiliating the officers and gave them a hard time. Set to work in a party of officers only, they had to do the same jobs as the men, even though very few were used to hard work. It was usual for some to get a beating for not working hard enough or found to be skiving.

In camp there was a Thai canteen split into separate parts, one for the Japs and one for the prisoners. It was mostly used by the Japs because they had the money. A private's pay was about a penny a day, NCO's pay was a little more, while an officer's pay was quite a bit more. The officers therefore were able to buy food to supplement their poor diet. They did make some contribution to the other ranks' mess fund and, with a small contribution from the men's pay, it was used to buy extra for Christmas Day. A small cow on its last legs was bought from the Thais outside the camp. The rest of the mess fund bought sugar, eggs, cooking oil, salt and spices.

The Japs gave us a day off work, for what was our first Christmas as prisoners of war. The cooks did a good job in the circumstances. With sugar in our tea, and meat flavouring our stew we thought it was lovely. They also produced a fried meat ball or as we called it, a "doo-fur." The day began with a service and ended with a concert, which got rid of the blues for a time. The concert was well staged, one act being a female impersonator called Bobby Spong. The lads loved him, and to us he looked like a real dolly bird. Everyone joined in with the favourite war songs accompanied by an accordionist and whatever musical instruments were possessed or had been made.

It was back to work the following day, but with spirits a little higher. One evening after work we were surprisingly called out on the parade ground to line up. Already feeling tired, we were called to attention. The Jap engineer officer in charge spoke in English to announce that many tools were missing so, until they were found, we would have to stay there. On that dark chilly night, standing to attention, with only some small part of our bodies covered, he said "All men, stand still and not talk and if mosquito come don't move." We stood there for what seemed like hours, tormented by insects, unable to move. Then eventually we were dismissed after it appeared that the tools had been found. We thought it was a case of not being able to count.

I had been lucky up to now really, with perhaps one or two bouts of malaria and dysentery. The dysentery was more distressing because it was impossible to keep clean. Without paper of any sort we made use of the broad leaves on the camp trees. Early in the month of January, our section of the railway embankment was finished, so a party was formed to move further up country. I was passed fit enough to go and we paraded one day with our kit and some stores, to march to our next camp. The weather had improved by now, as we marched along the track which we had worked upon. The track followed the River Kwai Noi, a busy river where often we saw large bamboo rafts skilfully navigated downstream by, at the most, two men. We passed others working their section of railway track which took us through cuttings in the rocks which other prisoners had blasted. Theirs was a hard job, having to chisel a hole a metre deep by hand for an explosive charge to blast away the rocks. Others broke the debris into small ballast for the track. Continuing through paddy fields and bamboo jungle in the hot sunshine, we arrived at the next camp, called Wun Lung.[29]

---

[29] Arrived 16th January

54

From Camp to Camp

We met up with a few Wun Lung lads we knew who were working on a stretch of embankment nearby. After spending just one night there, we had our early morning rice and watery vegetable soup, and lined up to be counted. When the Japs were satisfied that everyone was on parade, we moved off with our treasured small possessions. The jungle track took us to the next camp about ten miles up country, called Wun-Tu-Kin[30]. Arriving there, we were allowed the rest of the day to ourselves, which was spent clearing up the place, and ourselves.

Next morning, it was back to work on the railway, but this time collecting saws, axes, heavy hammers and steel chisels. It became obvious that the party in which I was selected was to be given work to do, different from embankment constructing. We were to cut down selected trees, then manhandle them to the spot where the railway was to cross a stream, culvert or dip in the track. To cut through a large tree with a cross cut saw, pushed and pulled by two men is not easy, especially in the weak condition most men were in by this time. But this turned out to be the easy part. When the trees were cut down, everyone lined up in twos on each side of the tree, placing a bamboo pole every two feet or more apart. After the tree trunk was rolled onto the poles, the command was given to take the strain and lift. Sometimes it came up evenly and without difficulty, other times, when someone didn't make much effort, down it went again with maybe pinched fingers or damaged feet or backs. This resulted in bangs across the face, arms or body from the guards for anyone handy. Some trees had to be carried quite a distance to the track. Sometimes elephants were used to pull the tree trunks, but occasionally they refused even though they were chopped on the

---

[30] Jack arrived at Wang Takhain in mid-January. On 21st February he transferred to Ban Kao.

forehead with a machete (axe). We would then have to move it in the usual way.

Some trunks were sawn off to length, then we stripped off the bark, and axed a slow tapered point on one end. These were the piles, and depending on the job to do, could be quite long. The piles were then driven into position by a primitively constructed on the spot timber frame, maybe twenty or more feet high, pyramid fashion, and a heavy weight roped over a pulley at the top. Heavier weights would have two ropes and pulleys extending in opposite directions. All men were called to pull on the ropes to bring up the weights slowly to the top. Then a sudden dash forward to slacken the rope and drop the weight with an abrupt thud. Two men generally guided the pile from a perched situation near the top. This was a slow punishing job, jolting your whole body when the weight suddenly dropped and the pile sank lower.

When all piles were positioned, the other trunks were barked, then axed all round into a straight square baulk, to be used as beams. This was extremely tiring work, standing astride the tree trunk and swinging the adze axe up and accurately down with both arms, gradually chipping away the wood to form a flat straight face. Some men would then secure them in position on the piles, as instructed, to form the main frame of the bridge, finishing off with main bracings.

I was involved with this kind of work until the twenty second of March 1943, when I was selected for a party to move farther up country to a camp called Rintin. This was quite a distance from the first camp at Chungkai. A dozen or more camps, following the course of the River Kwai Noi, were formed between Rintin and Chungkai. Some were small camps, but all had to be hacked out of the jungle and made habitable before railroad work could commence.

Each move from one camp to another meant losing friends. Therefore many men from the same unit were parted. Although Australian and Dutch prisoners occupied the same camps it was rare to work together.

IMPERIAL JAPANESE ARMY

I am interned in   *THAILAND*

My health is excellent.

~~I am ill in hospital.~~

~~I am working for pay.~~

I am not working

Please see that *ALL AT HOME*   is taken care

My love to you   *JACK*

So it was time to move and I remember the bad impression I got of
Rintin Camp on arrival. This may have been due to the fact that I
wasn't feeling very well. I had a pain in my lower right side. This
developed into an agonising pain during the night. It made me groan
and shout, which kept myself and others awake. Whatever it was, I

had to endure it until next morning, when the medical orderly in the hut called the camp doctor. He diagnosed appendicitis, and made a request to the Nips that I should be evacuated. After a long delay I found myself on a stretcher, with another prisoner ready on another stretcher, ready to be moved down to a base camp. Standing over us was a Nip soldier, holding a rifle with bayonet fixed. This, I thought, was my end, being so vulnerable lying there, and with the lingering thought that at the very least I was going to need an operation in this primitive place.

I was glad when at last we were carried down to the riverside to be put on a boat to be evacuated. When, in due course, we were taken off the boat and stretchered into the camp, it was a relief to find the camp was Chungkai. I was examined by the medical officer who told me I had renal colic, much to my relief. He gave me instructions and permission to go to the cookhouse and obtain six pints of boiled water a day to drink, besides drinks served up with meals. This was my treatment for ten days, until I was discharged. During those ten days I was able to take a well-earned rest from work, which helped me to regain strength. At this time, I somehow made good friends with the Thai assistants at the Thai canteen. Although I could not talk to them, they seemed to like me, and chat to one another about me. It emerged quite quickly that I was being called *Sing*. So whenever I caught the word, I became attentive.

Chungkai was a base camp with the huts for the many different complaints set away from the rest of the prisoners. Already in this large camp many men had died, and each day funeral parties were seen. They were replaced by more sick men brought in from the tortuous work and conditions of the Thai jungle camps. Apart from camp duties to make the camp clean, collect wood for the cookhouses, cookhouse duties, fetch water from the river and look after the sick, there was no other work. At least no hard work for the Nips. But everyone able to do something was given a job. It was a very industrious camp. After daily duties were performed, many rackets were started, making cigarettes with home-made gadgets, clog making as well as coffee and tea making. These were hawked around for sale to anyone with some money. The coffee was made by burning rice, but it was a change from cookhouse tea, which had no sugar or milk, just a weak looking grey liquid.

I made for myself one of the simple gadgets for rolling my own cigarettes. It consisted of two pieces of wood and a piece of canvas or cloth. We used book pages or writing paper to roll the cigarettes in. The writing paper was split into two thin sheets by lightly cutting across with a razor and peeling back.

My visits to the canteen nearly always resulted in being called to one side behind the counter to be given hot cooked food. By cookhouse standards it was tasty and nourishing, which enabled me to build up my stamina again. The only thing was, I had to make sure the Nips didn't see me. One of the Thai assistants, a lad of about twenty, asked me to wash his shorts and shirt out. He gave me soap for this, and maybe a little money. I can't remember exactly, but it was the extra food and friendship which I appreciated. The soap came in handy too, to wash my own few clothes. The river was the washing machine; the garments were bashed on the rocks to get the sweat and dirt out.

Great efforts were made to keep the morale of the camp at a good level. Occasionally a concert was put on, or a musical, or a play. The titles of a few spring to mind: "Wonderbar", "Bonnie Scotland", and "Night Must Fall". I helped to make the props for these. Some of the scripts were written to make fun of the Nips, and sometimes led to bashings when some Nips attending realised they were the victims of ridicule.

Health Problems

At one time in the camp, cholera struck. The victims were isolated in a hut away from the rest. No matter what your state of health, if cholera struck anyone it was death in a day or two. The risk was very high for the dedicated medical orderlies who worked night and day to do whatever was possible to give them a fighting chance. It was a regular daily occurrence to see three funeral parties, with five each time going down to the cremation site. It was a grim thought to weigh up the time it would take for all of us to be wiped out. Everything now had to be disinfected, and all drinking and eating utensils dipped in boiling water before meals. There was little that could be done for the patients, but I think we did eventually get some vaccine. It was a relief when the number of victims of cholera was reduced. However, it was a pitiful sight to see how other complaints had reduced once healthy British soldiers to just living skeletons.

Daily parties had to go on bamboo cutting for the cookhouse fuel. This meant long walks out of the camp with Nip guards. By this time many men were without boots, and mine were not very good. For a time I, like many others, went about barefoot, until I made myself a pair of wooden sandals. These were just pieces of wood cut to the shape of the foot, with a strap nailed on, to fit over the fore part of the foot. A lot of injuries to the feet were caused by the splinters of bamboo which lay everywhere the bamboo was growing. These scratches and cuts soon became infected and ulcers formed. It was on one of these bamboo parties that I had a cut on the back of my left leg from the sharp splinters of bamboo. An ulcer formed and grew rapidly. When I saw the medical officer, he told me to move into the Ulcer Ward of the hospital area. This hut, like all other huts in the camp, was about one hundred feet long, with a continuous stretch of bamboo slats to form a platform to lie on. There was a platform on either side and a space to walk between, which was six feet wide.

The platforms were two feet high. Each patient had about two and a half feet of space.

It became quite depressing to see that everyone to the left and right and opposite had ulcers. To leave my friends and go to a place amongst strangers was not very pleasant, but the sight of men reduced to little more than skeletons was frightening. Some had ulcers on both legs, and to make it worse no-one had a bandage to cover them up. The smell, day after day, was terrible. A medical officer came around each day, but had very little to offer for treatment. The first thing for the orderly to do when he came round was to use a spoon to scoop off the puss. This could be very painful, but he understood and did the job with a joke and a laugh. He had no proper dressings so all we had was a piece of tissue paper dipped in Permanganate of Potash placed on the ulcer. The problem for me was to keep it on until the next day, because it was on the back of my leg on the calf. The smell in the hut attracted big flies which settled on the ulcers of anyone asleep or too sick to knock them off. It was common to see maggots crawling and feeding on the puss oozing from the large areas of bad flesh.

SERVICE DES PRISONNIERS DE GUERRE

Name JENNINGS J.
Nationality BRITISH
Rank PRIVATE
Camp No. 2 P. O. W. Camp,
Thailand.

To:-
MISS L.M. MILLARD
4 CHERRY ORCHARD
OLD HILL
STAFFS.

PASSED
P.W. 5692

I was admitted to this Ulcer Ward on the twenty second of August 1943. Each day seemed a long depressing existence. Little wonder that many men passed away with very little hope of a quick recovery. The food hadn't much nourishment in it to sustain the fittest, let alone some of the weakest. It would have been nice to have received a letter from home or a Red Cross parcel, but even these were held by the Nips. Occasionally a little bit of cheerful news came to us, of the progress in some places of the Allied battles with the Germans and the Nips. Sometimes we heard the drone of Allied 'planes overhead and the dull thud of bombs dropping somewhere. Home made draughts and cards helped to pass the time away, and jokes were passed around from one to another until they were stale.

The treatment on my leg ulcer had little effect and it had grown to a large pear shape. The MO changed the treatment to *Binidine*, which is only a mild antiseptic. Gradually the ulcer seemed to improve slightly.

Our second Christmas in captivity had passed almost without notice, apart from a little extra to the usual rice and vegetable water. We had survived another monsoon season, which brought very heavy rains

IMPERIAL JAPANESE ARMY

Date *16ᵀᴴ JANUARY 1944*

Your mails (and ————) are received with thanks.
My health is (good, ~~usual~~, ~~poor~~).
~~I am ill in hospital.~~
~~I am working for pay (I am paid monthly salary).~~
I am not working.
My best regards to *YOUR AUNT LILY, GRANNIE AND*

FAMILY AND MOTHER AND ALL AT HOME

Yours ever,

Jack

and cold nights, with strong, gusty winds. Now, in early 1944, it was almost two years since the capitulation of Singapore. The news we received was more encouraging, and there was a slight improvement in the meals, though we still had rather disgusting stuff sometimes. The hygiene in the camp had improved by now, so the death rate had dropped. Before I knew it, it was my twenty fourth birthday. There was an Australian, twenty one years old, lying next to me who had leg ulcers. He was not very strong-willed and gradually lost all interest. It was depressing to find that he had died right beside me one day.

I had encouraging news from the MO, who said that if my ulcer continued to improve the way it had, I would be able to have a skin graft. It was still large, but the colour had changed to a healthier looking pink except for one or two high spots. These high spots were treated with Bluestone to burn them off level. When all was ready, the time came for me to have the skin graft.

With great relief I was moved to the surgical unit from the depressing, smelly hut of the ulcer ward. The surgical hut, although the same construction as all the rest, was cleaner and more cheerful.

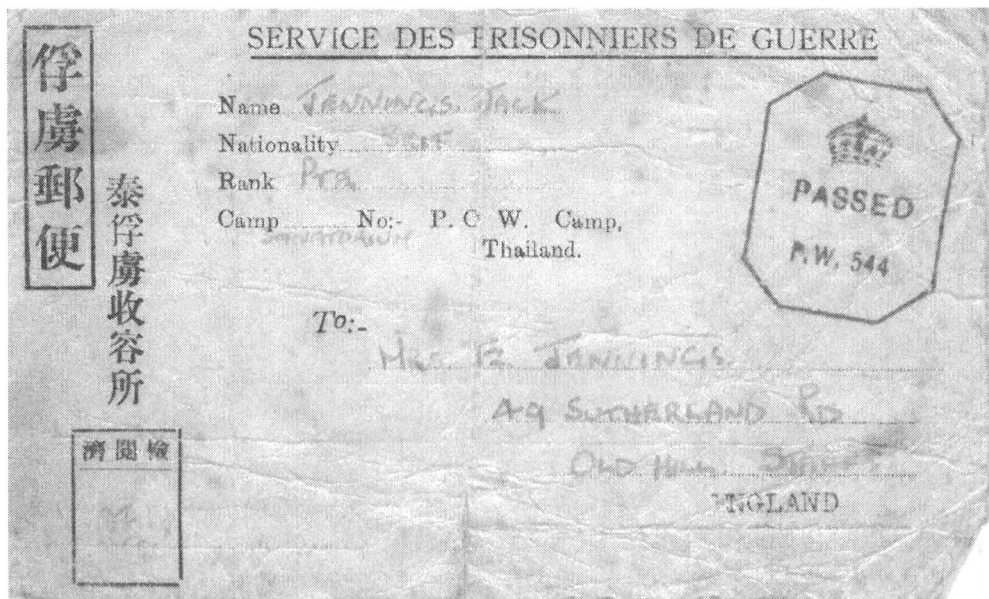

SERVICE DES PRISONNIERS DE GUERRE

Name Jennings Jack

Nationality

Rank Pte

Camp No:- P. O W. Camp,
Thailand.

PASSED
P.W. 544

To:-

Mrs. B. Jennings.

49 Sutherland Rd.

Old Hill

ENGLAND

The MO, whose name was Captain Sykes, came to me to tell me what he was going to do. The operating table, like everything else, was made with bamboo. It was soon my turn to be on it. There was no anaesthetic to put me to sleep, just an injection to begin with then, to my horror, a six inch long needle was put into my spine. I saw all the rest happen. The skin on my thigh was lifted with tweezers and cut round to take off pieces about as big as peas. These were transferred to the ulcer. This was repeated twenty five times. With dressings on thigh and leg, the operation was complete.

Day after day the doctor and orderlies worked tirelessly and cheerfully doing their jobs, with very few medical supplies issued from the Nips. Without real hospital comforts, like a spring mattress, the bamboo slat sleeping platforms caused sores, of which I was a victim. It took several more weeks for all the sores to heal, and on the twenty eighth of May '44, I was discharged to unite with the so-called fit of my unit in camp. It had been more than nine months since I was admitted to the ulcer ward, and camp life had seemed to improve in some ways.

The Nips were as worried about the flies in camp as we were, so they

IMPERIAL JAPANESE ARMY

Date 2-6-44

Your mails (and   ) are received with thanks.
My health is (good, usual, poor).
I am ill in hospital.
I am working for pay (I am paid monthly salary).
I am not working.
My best regards to MoTHeR   NARY   TRaVis. IRIS,

           WiLsG, BeNT, Ja K, & HaR oRiBt

                    Yours ever,

ordered everyone to catch a certain number of flies each day, and parade to hand them in. It was comical to see men visiting the latrines with a fly swatter, swatting and collecting their quota of big bluebottles.

The Nip Camp Officer one day told us we should keep fit, which of course was easy for them, eating all our Red Cross food. He instructed us to file through his hut to watch him do his exercises. This was a humiliating exercise, demonstrating how fit we should be when everyone passing by his bed was a living skeleton. Sometimes an inspection by a Nip officer was announced with very little warning. Everyone who could move outside the hut did so, while the Nips checked all the kits and took away pens or pencils, paper resembling a diary and anything which suited them. They looked especially for hidden radios or parts. On one occasion the Nip Medical Officer came round, but not to observe what help he could arrange for our health or hygiene. He was only interested in our private parts. Everyone sat on the bedspace with legs apart waiting for their turn for inspection. When he had gone, the lads' comments would not have pleased him much, for we saw it as a stupid humiliating visit.

The Nips tried to humiliate us and treat us as if we had done something terrible to offend them. A few of them we found to be reasonable, but the majority were unpredictable and some had fiery tempers. Not many prisoners escaped being hit at some time. I was walking through the camp one day and saw a Nip approaching. I saluted him, as was the order, but he replied by just smacking me in the face. I turned round as he passed by but he just walked on as if nothing had happened. They had very little respect for sick men, as in their view it was a crime to be sick. One day in particular I remember. We were on a rice loading party in the railway station sidings a few months after the railway had been completed, connecting Bangkok in Thailand to Moulmein in Burma. The Nips by that time had suffered defeats in Burma, with many casualties. The wounded soldiers were transported from Burma by the railway that we had built. The job at the station was for us to carry the rice sacks from the train to motor trucks for distribution. This was a very hard job for fit men, but in our weak state it was heavy going to carry large sacks without a rest. On this particular day there were wounded Nip soldiers in the rail trucks or hobbling on crutches or sticks nearby. They looked a pitiful, dejected lot of sick troops. The guards in charge of us sought to humiliate them, their own fellow countrymen, by taking the rice sacks and running with them. They just laughed and jeered at them as they passed. If they had been our wounded, we would have given them cigarettes and chatted to them, but not our Nip guards, they never went near them. Their mentality never told them that the more rice sacks they carried, the less we would have left to carry.

There were parties coming and going at this time, some going to Japan, many coming in from the camps in the north – all in extremely poor health. There was a camp which we were told we would be going to, called *Nak Kom Paton*, between Chungkai and Bangkok. It was supposed to be a rest camp with better conditions. I was soon in a party to go there with a few of the lads I knew. It was a new camp, but the huts were very much the same, except that wooden boards replaced the bamboo slats. This was much more comfortable to lie on. However we soon found out that the bugs, lice and ants were still as plentiful. In the daytime we often watched the contest between ants and bugs: the ants chased the bugs and carried them off when we killed them. The smell from this was awful. The food there was slightly better and so were the medical resources. In this camp I clearly remember a fenced-off compound for the mentally sick and shell-shocked men, who roamed about playing like children, with things made especially for them. Once, not long ago, they had been strong, fit fighting men, who had seen all the harsh realities of war, and prison camp life, in incredibly atrocious conditions, made worse by slaving long hours of work on a railway in all weathers, and without enough food in quality and quantity. There was one prisoner whom I recognised. He had been with me in our platoon up to being taken prisoner. I called him by his name to come to the fence, but he didn't even remember it. At least he had survived and maybe would return home.

The favourite pastimes in this camp, where, for a change, we didn't have any work to do for the Nips, were playing chess, draughts, cards and chatting to anyone, especially old comrades who were worse off than yourself. There was one soldier in our hut, who had lost a leg, who was a good chess player. He regularly played six men at the same time, making a move at one board, then hopping on one leg up or down the hut to the next player. Following round in this manner he would move, hop and sit for long periods. This camp gave me an opportunity to carve my own chess set. With only a penknife, I painstakingly carved the complete set from wood picked up in camp. As I was carving the sixteen pawns, I showed my progress to a fellow platoon pal who still had big ulcers. He asked if he could help to carve one or two for me to pass the time. He was so pleased when I said "Yes." His gallant effort at matching mine were not quite what I expected, although I did praise him and thank him. One half of the set was darkened with Permanganate of Potash from the medical corporal. In due course I also made an octagonal chess table which was put to very good use. The table stayed with me from camp to camp after that, until it became too much of a burden. The chess set remained with me until the end of the war, when I was able to bring it home, including the few carved by my old pal Sid.

Showing off my chess set to a press photographer, 1995.

At this point of the story, Jack's recollection differs from documentary evidences. According to his Liberation Questionnaire and the diary of Major David Nixon, Jack travelled north on the Death Railway to Linson on September 18th 1944 (See Appendix 7). Jack has no recollection of this and is certain that he went straight on to the 'old' State Railway.

Back to Work

Everyone who went to this camp may have thought it was a rest camp until our release, but that was a mistake. By that time the Nips were taking a beating in Burma and the railway was put to good use transporting troops and stores back and forth. Therefore, the Nips required groups of men to maintain the track and cut timber for fuel for the engines. After a few months' rest in that camp, I was on the move again in a wood cutting party. We were taken somewhere up in the jungle to a small camp. The railway for which we were to cut the wood to fuel the engines was the old Thai State Railway going to the Burma border in the north, not the railway which we had built. We were more isolated than ever. The job was to work in twos, select a tree, and with an axe and a double handed crosscut saw, cut down, trim and cut into half-metre lengths. Then, anything more than about seventy millimetres across had to be chopped and stacked until the stack was one metre high and two metres long. Imagine fifteen or more pairs of men all competing to find the easiest trees to cut, and the ones nearest to the railway track. All the stacks of wood had to be stacked in line, close to the track. When your stack had been checked as being to the required daily two metres by one, you could sit and wait for the others to finish. A lot depended on luck, whether your allotted axe and saw were sharp, and whether your judgement of an easy tree to saw and chop was good. Then again it depended on the distance from the track that you had to go to find those trees. Each day, of course, it became farther into the jungle away from the track. It was a hard back-breaking job and a difficult daily task. The slowest groups were seen by the Nips as idle, so they quite frequently got a beating with sticks or rifles. On one occasion I slung the axe until my back gave way. With a Nip standing next to me I feared the worst, but luckily he had watched me get slower and slower and knew it was genuine. He was maybe one of the better ones.

This was the pattern of events for quite a while to come. When we had cut sufficient for that area we moved to a camp farther north. The jungle was sometimes very dense so it was necessary to make a mark on the trees with an axe to find your way back, from excursions to find water, or any other reason. We never knew when we would come across a wild animal or snake. The Nips occasionally shot a wild animal to help the supply of food, which was scarce for them, as well as us, in the small camps that we worked from. We, of course, only got the left overs after they had the choicest pieces. We also had to search for and cook anything found in the jungle that was edible. Without the extra vitamins we got through our own initiative, there would have been more sickness and deaths. It was an extremely lonely place to be in that part of Thailand, cut off from any outside help. The nights, from dusk to dawn, were at times very frightening, sometimes because of strange sounds, at other times because of strong monsoon winds and rain. It was necessary at times for everyone to get up in the night to hold the hut up. Several men would lean on the centre support bamboo poles to counter the force of the winds.

One day, out on the working party, I was given the job of sharpening the saws. It was a change from the job of cutting and chopping trees and much easier. The job became regular each day for some time, but it kept me fully occupied because everybody wanted a sharp saw. I first had to find two small trees close together and cut them to a suitable height with a notch on top to hold the crosscut saw rigid while it was filed. At first, when the files were good, the job was alright, but as the files wore, the pressure exerted had to be more, so my fingers became sorer. It was like getting blood out of a stone to get a new file.

Going out to our place of work one morning we found leaflets hidden for us to find. They had been dropped by Allied 'planes at night, and collected and placed discretely for us. The cheerful news told us that the war in Europe was nearly over, and Japan was as jittery as the Germans. We were very happy to hear this news but we couldn't show our happiness, nor even let the Nips know about the leaflets. A

TO ALL BRITISH SOLDIERS!

The war in Europe is nearly over. Germany has met a succession of hard blows. She is now groggy on her feet and the knockout is due soon.

Ten weeks after British and American troops invaded France we took Paris. More than a quarter of France is now ours and Allied armies have been pushed in from the north and the south. The French themselves have risen and, supplied with Allied arms, are fighting the Germans.

Italy, Germany's ex-partner, is three quarters occupied. We have already taken Rome and Florence.

In the Balkans Roumania has come over on our side. She is the first of the slave states to do so. Others look as if they will follow.

Russian troops are on German soil in East Prussia. Germany is finished—and knows it.

In Asia we are doing well now.

We will do better still when Germany is out and more ships and arms and men are released.

In Burma 50,000 Japanese soldiers have been killed this year. We have beaten the Jap on three fronts.

In the Pacific our Fleet—already double the size of the Japanese fleet and still growing—has isolated dozens of Japanese garrisons. Saipan has been taken giving us a base 1,200 miles from the Japanese mainland.

The Americans have started daylight bombing raids on Japan.

Japan is as jittery as Germany. The tide has turned in earnest.

TAKE HEART. WE ARE COMING!

South-East Asia Command.

punishment would have ensued if any of us had been caught with one. I took the risk and took care of it to take it home. From now on the news was good for us and served as a tonic.

Whenever we thought we had something to be happy about, the Nips nearly always seemed to sense it, and turned the screw a little bit harder. They enjoyed finding some excuse to punish certain individuals, severely bashing them and then putting them in a confined cage with little food and water. As the air raids by the Allies got closer their tempers worsened. In one camp about this time, we were set a task to dig a trench in front of our hut. This, they said, was to take cover from the air-raids. The width of the trench was two metres and it stretched the length of the hut. From this work and news received, as well as intuition, we guessed we were digging our own graves.

(From this point on, Jack could be describing his move from the Thai-Burma Line to the State railway)

It was with great relief to find that we were going to move to another camp away from that sinister camp. I remember marching out of this

73

camp with my few possessions, the heaviest of which was the chessboard table, dismantled and tied up under my arm. No-one ever knew how far we would have to walk whenever we moved. I reluctantly had little choice, before very long, to sling the table into the jungle, as it was an unnecessary burden. I would have loved to have been able to keep it.

Our party was quite small by this time as we moved yet further north doing our usual job of wood-cutting from small camps. The pressure on us to work hard grew less as we sensed that the war must have been going in our favour. Then we heard the rumour that the war in Europe was over. It was a great talking point which brought happier faces all round. That was until we realised it would make very little difference to us. Our hopes were high whenever we thought our time must come when the Nips were defeated and we would be able to get away from this inhospitable jungle of Thailand and our hated captors.

In all the years as a prisoner, I only received a sixth of a Red Cross parcel on two occasions. We were only allowed to send two or three printed messages home, and I only received one or two letters, the last dated 1944.

End of the War

A few months passed, and rumours came around that the war was finished with Japan as well as Germany. Then on August the Twenty Fifth 1945, we picked up leaflets which had been dropped to confirm our beliefs. The Nip guards must have known too because they allowed us to rest more than work. They sat down amongst us and tried to talk and show how much English they had learnt. The cries of "Speedo" had stopped, being replaced by "Yasume" (to rest). Finally, in that remote camp close to Uttaradit, near a small village or kampong, our officer-in-charge gave us the official confirmation speech to tell us that we were free and that the war was over. He told us to keep calm and behave like good British soldiers and not to stray far from camp. We would be allowed to wander into the kampong for brief periods.

In our small party was at least one man belonging to the same battalion as me. His home town was West Bromwich and his name was Lance Jones, of Welsh descent. Naturally everyone called him Taffy. He and I paired off together for our first step out to freedom to wander around the kampong. We didn't have much money to spend, but that didn't matter much because we were so happy to feel free again. The Thais were so friendly to us, even though we couldn't understand their language, their faces were all smiles and they cheered us up with kind actions. We must have looked a very pitiful and strange lot of human beings to them, being so scantily dressed, half-starved and needing medical attention. They, like us, were so pleased to know that the war was over and the Nips would not harass them anymore.

As we strolled into the kampong we came to a small bamboo kiosk where jewellery was on display. It wasn't the jewellery, but the delightful smiling faces of the two young Thai girls which attracted us. We stopped and to our great surprise and pleasure they both

75

TO ALL ALLIED PRISONERS OF WAR

THE JAPANESE FORCES HAVE SURRENDERED UNCONDITIONALLY AND THE WAR IS OVER

WE will get supplies to you as soon as it is humanly possible and we will make arrangements to get you out. Because of the distances involved it may be some time before we can achieve this.

YOU will help us and yourselves if you act as follows :

1. Stay in your camp until you get further orders from us.

2. Start preparing nominal rolls of personnel giving the fullest particulars.

3. List your most urgent necessities.

4. If you have been starved and underfed for long periods do not eat large quantities of solid food, fruit or vegetables at first. It is dangerous for you to do so. Small quantities at frequent intervals are much safer and will strengthen you far more quickly.

   For those who are really ill or very weak fluids such as broths and soups, making use of the water in which rice and other foods have been boiled, are much the best.

   Gifts of food from the local population should be cooked. We want to get you back home quickly, safe and sound, and we do not want you to risk getting diarrhoea, dysentery and cholera at this last stage.

5. Local authorities and/or Allied officers will take charge of your affairs in a very short time. Be guided by their advice.

SPE/1

76

spoke perfect English. Speaking in high pitched, musical tones it was fascinating to hear them talk. They told us that both were students at Bangkok University, studying medicine, hoping to become doctors. One was called Somporn, and the other one's name was Som Sri. We exchanged addresses and promised to write when we arrived home in England. That short friendship was just what we needed to raise our spirits, after our long arduous battle against ill treatment and ill health that we suffered in captivity.

We waited patiently day after day, wondering when the announcement would come to tell us we would be moving back to a more realistic state of freedom. The leaflets which had been dropped on the 25th August told us to

Somporn

stay in camp, prepare nominal rolls of personnel, not to eat large quantities of food, fruit or vegetables at first, and gifts of food from local people should be cooked. Allied officers would take charge in a very short time. This advice was taken by me, but not by everyone; I survived, thankfully.

On the Second of September our prayers were answered with the announcement that we should quickly prepare ourselves for a move. With shouts of joy and some doubt at such an incredible change of circumstances, we assembled with our few possessions. We left camp to go the short distance to the railway track and waiting trucks, with the Japanese giving orders as usual. Waving cheerfully to the local Thais, we climbed aboard and moved slowly away, never to see the girls Somporn and Som Sri again.

We shook and bumped along for many miles, through what appeared then to be lovely countryside, the Nips still keeping quiet. We eventually slowed down to a halt and the Nips dismounted and walked forward. In a short time they came back with two Allied

Anong, Nong-Yong, Seripit

officers. We continued our journey until we stopped again. The first stage of our return home was at a place called Lopburi. We were ordered off the trucks and marched to the town where we were allocated our sleeping quarters in a large building like a school. After settling in we had a meal cooked by the local Thais - more rice of course. The Nip guards were still with us: when would we shake them off? At least they couldn't do anything to us any more, not with two armed Allied officers. We were allowed to go out into the village afterwards for a few hours.

My pal and I first watched some Thai men playing Russian Pool in a small games room for a while, and then nearby we met an English speaking young girl in a ladies' clothes shop. She asked us to meet her other two sisters in the shop. The elder one who owned the shop was probably around thirty and didn't speak much English. Her name was Anong, so the shop was called Anong's Shop. The next youngest sister was a teacher in a kintergarden. Her name was Seripit. The youngest one was about eighteen and a student. Both of these younger sisters were able to talk well in English, so we were able to catch up with the news, and tell them how pleased we were for them, and us, that the war was over. The youngest one, whose name was Nong-Yong said they would see us before we left.

We stayed no more than two nights in Lopburi before we continued our long journey home. The whole town seemed to be around to see us assemble in the centre of the village, but the three sisters found us to wish us a safe journey, and thank us for our short friendship. The youngest one brought her bike to carry my few possessions on it to the railway. It was goodbye to Lopburi on the next stage towards Bangkok, with a grand send off.

For the past three and a half years our travels in Thailand had been mostly on foot, when we were unfit to go anywhere let alone work afterwards. To be travelling by rail or road was a luxury to us.

By the late afternoon we found ourselves led into new surroundings in a camp near Bangkok called *Pratchai*. It was the Fourth of September when we set foot in this hospital camp, where we finally considered ourselves free, and in the caring hands of British medical staff who were geared up and keen to see us recover and be fit enough to continue home. The three-day journey from Uttaradit had been about 270 miles. We had finally shaken off our guards; they left us unnoticed; what a relief that was. At last we were able to have a good clean up and dump any unwanted things. By far the best news was that we could write a letter to our family. This is a copy of my very first letter to my fiancée, Mary:

4th September '45

My Darling Sweetheart,

This is the letter I have been waiting for:- for the last 3½ years of which I have been a prisoner of war. This opportunity has been given to us by our own officers, who are now completely in charge of us, and to whom we were handed over to this day at Pratchai camp, which is near to Bangkok.

Well my dearest, how are you feeling now? -- If you are as happy as I am, and feeling well, you must be looking really fine: Now it won't be long before both our dreams are realized! as you remarked in one of your letters. ---Hold tight darling I am on the way!

As you will have probably learnt, I and all of us here expect to be flown home all the way. This may be in a few days' time, when things are a bit more organized. I am all in favour of this experience to add to my many experiences these last 3½ years, which I will have more time to relate later on.

We heard the war was over on the 16th August, but the Nips did not leave us, and we were confined to our billets, until one day leaflets were dropped by a plane, telling us that the war was over, and we were free. That was about ten days ago. Since then, the Nips

79

had very little to do with us, we took no notice of them and wandered into the village where the Thai people were most hospitable; it was almost unbelievable. On the second of September, we began our freedom journey, and from that day we have had a grand reception from the Thai people. They are very, very kind, and ask for our addresses, Thai students especially, who can talk some English.

Now we are in a large building, waiting for the next big journey. I don't think you need worry now. I think you can get the Christmas dinner ready for one more this year without a doubt. I will write more details of moving later, I just want to make you feel content, and satisfied that I am O.K. When or if we are given an address, I will let you know, so that you can reply.

Now I will say goodbye darling, all my love to you, and will see you soon.

Cheerio Sweetheart

Yours ever

Jack

xxxxx

xxxxxx

xxxxxxx

At Pratchai we had a few days' rest, which gave us the chance to adjust to the more humane way of living. Some of the men were very sick and needed medical care and would have to stay there awhile, but those fit enough to travel by air were selected and put on standby. I was lucky enough to be able to travel, so on the Eighth of September we were put into groups of about twenty five and given a group number. We had a bath or shower, a meal and then waited to be called. When the 'planes were ready for us, we were taken to the airfield by lorry to be in readiness for our alloted plane. The R.A.F. lads in charge at the airfield told us we would be flying to Rangoon, which to me was a bit of a disappointment. I was expecting to fly home, but at least it was a start. When our group was called we walked to the waiting 'plane. It was a Dakota, a small 'plane which

80

had been used for bombing raids, not a luxury 'plane for us. Fitted with a type of twin bucket seats each side, and with small circular windows, it didn't impress us much. We boarded and waited for one of the most important days of our lives. With a great roar we took off and soared above the airfield, giving us a good view of the land where we had suffered so much hardship and misery. At least we had made it. There were many fellow prisoners who had died, and many who would still not make it. To have gone through hell for three and a half years was cruel, but to be cheated from survival at the last moment was really cruel luck.

As we climbed higher we shook as we negotiated turbulent weather. The aircrew were instructed to fly low because of our condition, but they had no alternative with the weather conditions. We felt the cold and shivered at that altitude although the medical orderly gave us blankets. The crew didn't seem to be affected at all in their shirt sleeves. After about three hours and seven hundred miles of flying we landed safely in Rangoon.

Here we were quickly whisked off in waiting ambulances to the Reception Centre into the care of British nurses and the W.V.S. We were soon seated at tables for a meal. This really was luxury, with chairs and tables the likes of which we hadn't seen for so long. To be waited on, and receive a genuine English meal, with a knife, fork and spoon, had us all excited. What a reception! The meal over, we were then taken to a Centre which was specially prepared for Allied prisoners to rehabilitate before the next step towards home. Another great welcome with cups of tea and cigarettes, and then to our beds for complete bliss, with a soft mattress, white sheets and pillows. We were then issued with clean new clothes, our own knife, fork and spoon, a new pay book and some money. Another meal was laid on before returning to our beds in the attendance of British nurses. Clean pyjamas, airmail letters and pencils awaited us. It was overwhelming. Was it all real, or a dream? It was indeed real, as we settled down to a comfortable night's sleep without bugs, lice, mosquitoes and all the other torments of prisoner of war life in Thailand.

The morning after, a medical officer came round with the duty nurse

RECOVERED PRISONERS OF WAR
ON ACTIVE SERVICE.

BY AIR MAIL.

ADDRESS ONLY.

POSTAGE
FREE.

MISS E JENNINGS
49 SUTHERLAND ROAD
OLD HILL
STAFFS ENGLAND

CABLE C AND W WIRELESS LIMITED
"Via Imperial"

telegram contains the following particulars in the order named
essage, Office of Origin, Number of Words, Date, Time handed in

CABLE AND WIRELESS LIMITED
OFFICE OF ISSUE
12 SEP. 1945
ADDRESS ON BACK

Time Received X 7700 CONFIRMATION

/P RANGOON JOSEPH

NGS 49 SUTHERLAND RD OLD

HILL STAFFS =

INDIA
ARRIVED SAFELY AT WRITING *
HOPE BE HOME SOON *
ADDRESS LETTERS AND TELEGRAMS TO

C/O P O BOX 164 LONDONEC1

JACK JENNINGS

ANY ENQUIRY RESPECTING THIS TELEGRAM SHOULD BE
MADE AT ANY OF THE COMPANY'S OFFICES

DEAR,

I AM NOW FREE AND IN SAFE HANDS.

I HOPE TO BE WITH YOU SOON.

MY ADDRESS IS :—

C/O RECOVERED P W MAIL CEN
BANGKOK
INDIA COMMAND

Date _____   Signature _____

to examine us and prescribe treatments, as necessary. We had to say what illness, injury or sickness we had endured. Whether we would be allowed to move freely or be detained under strict observation depended upon the result of the assessment of our fitness. My worst days as a prisoner were now passed, so when we were permitted to go to the cinema I was quite thrilled. One afternoon, we saw our first film for at least four years, a lovely film called "Going My Way," starring Bing Crosby. This was only eight days after we started our freedom journey from Utteradit in Northern Thailand.

Copy of letter sent from Rangoon:

I am now well on my way back home dearest being in hospital for rest at Rangoon. Two days ago I flew by plane from Bangkok, and believe me honey I enjoyed every bit of the journey. It was like riding in a bus. We now have every comfort here, good food, plenty of cigarettes, picture shows in attendance of English nurses, a lovely bed, just like home. It's hardly believable, only a week ago I was living in Thailand and still eating rice. Now we're on European food, and it's grand. I saw my first film for four years this afternoon, it was "Going my way" by Bing Crosby. Well darling I shall sure be glad to see you, after being apart for so long. I hope to be with you next month and we will sure have a big reunion. Thank you so much for

Telephone : MAYFAIR 9400.

Your Ref._____

W.O. Ref. SS/330/120/*141*
(Cas.P.W.)

THE WAR OFFICE,

CURZON STREET HOUSE,
CURZON STREET,
LONDON, W.1.

17·9·45·

~madam,

I am directed to inform you with pleasure that official information has been received that your *son·*

5830446 Pte J. Jennings The Suffolk Regiment· previously a prisoner of war in Japanese hands, has been recovered and is now with the Allied Forces.

The repatriation of recovered prisoners of war is being given highest priority, but it will be appreciated that some time must elapse before they reach the United Kingdom. Information of a general character regarding these recovered prisoners, including their movements before they reach home, will be given from time to time on the wireless and will be published in the press.

I am, ~madam,

Your obedient Servant,

C.H. Weeton.

Mrs E. Jennings.
49. Southerland Rd.
Old Hill.
Staffs.

all the mail you have sent and which I have received. It has done good work in keeping the smile you always wish to see, but you most probably understand I have had to cast away many thoughts of you, and home because in circumstances it was not fitting. Nevertheless I am now thinking of you always and am longing to be with you and make you happy. We will soon make up for the time we have lost. When I get home I am going to ask you to get married, I am sure you are longing for the same, aren't you? I should like to get your answer on this. I still love you, even more than ever, and I know we shall be happy.

There is every good prospect to look forward to:- I am sure darling I have no photo of you here. I should love to see one again before I see you personally. Will you try and get one for me. There are many friends here, Jack Jones whom I have not seen for 18 months, and Horace Smith who lives in Old Hill, and many others. I have no more space now so I will say goodbye darling. Best wishes for a happy reunion, and lots and lots of love.

I remain

Yours devotedly

Jack

x x x x x x x x

The next stage of our long journey back home came into reality after several more days of careful nursing. We were given a choice of going home the short way or the long way. The short way was by boat to Ceylon, now Sri Lanka, then through the Suez Canal and Mediterranean back to England. The long way was south to Australia to recuperate, before the journey homewards. For some it had to be the long way, for me it was the short and quickest way.

The embarkation day came[30]. We were driven down to the docks where our ship the *S.S. Orduna* was waiting. We boarded and were shown to our cabins, which were to be our floating homes for the next few weeks. We were given a chance to write home again, which we hoped would convey back to our families our love and hopes for the future.

We set sail westwards into the Indian Ocean, which we had navigated four years ago on the outward journey to Singapore to be rushed into combat and capitulation. I remembered it was the Indian Ocean where I threw my harmonica overboard after playing it often and blowing it out. There was more good food, relaxation, exercise and every comfort as we made steady progress in warm weather.

---

[30] 20th September

Eventually we came into port in Colombo, where we were allowed ashore. This was another different but pleasant experience where I was able to walk around the bazaars to barter and purchase a ruby necklace for Mary, and an ebony carving of an elephant, sandwiched by a matchbox holder and an ashtray, on an ebony stand with ivory decoration. Although the stop at Columbo was a short one, there was not much more to recall, as we couldn't go far away from the ship. In a day or two we set sail to enjoy again the life of luxury in comparison to the way we had been living. Many had by now put on some weight, now that the food was more like good food cooked tastily. The fresh air, too, was a tonic to us after experiencing stinking vegetation and rotten flesh in the ulcer huts. Out on deck we could rest and enjoy the sunshine, instead of slaving in hot sunshine and humid air. We also had a chance to write home again.

Sailing on into the Gulf of Aden, we made a brief call at Aden, before continuing through the Red Sea to Suez. There we waited for the pilot to navigate us through the Canal. That was a memorable experience in many ways. The war hadn't been over two months; it was the Eighth of October when we arrived at Suez. The canal had been blocked off from any shipping previously by sunken ships, but at that time a channel had been made to enable some ships to pass. There were still some wrecks visible, as we progressed very slowly into some very narrow parts of the Canal. Everyone was on deck to see the ship being carefully navigated by the very skilled Egyptian pilot. To our great relief we reached the northern end at Port Said safely, and without a bump.

After the pilot had gone ashore, we sailed on to the glorious calm of the beautiful blue Mediterranean Sea. It was quite a contrasting experience to be stretched out on deck enjoying the sunshine each day, with the boat moving along steadily like a swan on a lake. It was a complete contrast to cast our minds back to October 1941 when we crossed the Atlantic, when the waves were enormous, and the boat dropped and rose forty feet.

When we were one day issued with the normal warm clothing of battledress tunic and trousers it gave us a reminder that we should soon prepare ourselves for colder weather. Sailing then to the Bay of

Biscay, cooler strong winds and choppy seas prompted us to start counting the days to when we would be back home. The order came for us to change from tropical kit to our new issue, and then we were given an estimate of the day of arrival back in Liverpool. As we arrived near the mouth of the Mersey other boats signalled a welcome home with flags and hooters. Then it seemed ages before we could actually dock and tie up.

Mrs. E. Jennings 49 Sutherland Rd
Old Kill St J

Arrived safely see you soon
J Jenning

49 Sutherland Rd

Arrive New St 1-50 Fri
Jack

Home Again

It was the Twentieth of October, four years, almost to the day, since we had sailed from Liverpool, on the first leg of our journey which ended up with us landing in Singapore. We were so happy to be going ashore to a great welcome, the war was over and we had come through it all. The first thing I did was to send a telegram home to say I had arrived safely back in Liverpool. We had some pay and a travel warrant for the free train ride back home, so the railway station was the point we so eagerly made for next. After checking the time of the next train and time of arrival in New Street, Birmingham, I sent another telegram to say we were due in at 1.50 pm. I tried to imagine what it would be like when we arrived at Birmingham. Would anyone be there to meet me, and who? Then I thought, what would I look like to them? And would I see any change in them?

The great moment arrived, one of the greatest in my life. We arrived at New Street Station to great cheers and excitement. Gathering my kit together as quickly as possible, I hurried along the platform looking eagerly to see if anyone had come to meet me. Any friends I had travelled with were soon left behind as I spotted my mother and girlfriend joyfully coming my way, waving for my attention. Words did not come easy to any of us, as we met we flung our arms around one another. On the spot quite quickly was a Birmingham newspaper photographer. He asked my name and address and that of my sweetheart, and then took our photos. Next morning our photo was in the newspaper, minus my mother, much to her disappointment.

A car was hired to take us from the station back to Old Hill and home to an enormous welcome from neighbours who had put up flags and bunting. A special large sign had the message "Welcome Home, Jack." I was home at last, to meet the rest of the family and a great reunion party.

I had sailed 35,000 miles, travelled hundreds of miles on land and about 700 miles by air, all I wanted to do now was to settle down and wait for my demob. My mother cooked a rice pudding for me for my

Thirty Birmingham Ex-P.o.W.s Come Home

FATHERS, mothers, wives, and sweethearts crowded on to New-street Station, Birmingham, on Saturday afternoon to welcome home their prisoner - of - war sons, husbands, and relatives who recently arrived at Liverpool on the ex-P.o.W. ship Orduna from the Far East.

Among the repatriated prisoners who were on the train were 30 Birmingham men, including:

Cpl. Jack Medlicott, Phillips-street, Aston; Driver John Gardner, 42, Worldsend-avenue, Quinton; Lieut. R. Power, 109, Durham - road, Sparkhill; Pte. Ernest Saunders, 13/90, Lichfield-road, Aston; L.-Cpl. Evan Jones, 14, Downing-street, Handsworth and Pte. Jack Jennings, 29, Southern-road, Old Hill.

The Red Cross welcomed the returned prisoners and provided refreshments for those who were continuing their journey southward.

The Orduna brought 313 officers and other ranks besides a number of the Royal Marines and civilians.

The picture above was taken while the prisoners were enjoying cups of tea at New-street Station. Those below show three of the many happy reunions.

Pte. Ernest Saunders, of Aston, being greeted by his brother, Mr. Arthur Saunders.

L/Cpl. Evan Jones, of Handsworth, with his wife at New-street Station.

Pte. Jack Jennings, of Old Hill, with his sweetheart, Miss Lillian Millard, of 4, Cherry Orchard-road, Old Hill.

Mrs. Scribbans   Young People   Elgar Symphony

first dinner at home, which amused the rest of my family, knowing that rice had been, for the last three and a half years, our daily main food supply. Most of the Far East prisoners came back home looking thinner and undernourished. Nearly everyone had some injury to health or body, and all were noticeably yellow. We had to fill in a form to state what illnesses or other disabilities we had suffered. I received a small pension and was classed as disabled for some time. Then, after a while, I was sent for reassessment at Wolverhampton and declared no longer eligible for a disablement pension. To my disgust it was my own panel doctor who was the assessor.

For the time spent on active service during the four years up to our return to England in October 1945, we were granted six months leave. We had pay warrants sent to us to cash at the Post Office. A lump sum was sent for the period up to our release as prisoners, and from when we were taken prisoners. This army pay was paid only at the same rate as we received before capture. The rate of pay for the forces during those three and a half years had risen sharply for those fortunate enough not to have our bad luck. We therefore feel cheated by the Government for that pay freeze, which in the first place was caused by the dreadful disaster of sending us on a one-sided, impossible task.

The six month's leave meant that we would have to stay in the army for that period at least, and we had already served six years, all of which, of course, was compulsory. It was quite a slice out of life, at the most important time, and I felt it was not possible to achieve what I would have wished.

The most important thing on my mind then was to get married to my sweetheart who had so lovingly awaited my return. It was just a few weeks after, that I proposed. She accepted, and the marriage was arranged for the twenty second of December. My mother, unaware of our plan to marry, began to make plans for the best Christmas ever. I had to say "Sorry Mother, but we are going to get married three days before." In one way my mother was disappointed, but also she was quite happy with our decision to marry. She was going to lose a son so quickly, but she was gaining a lovely daughter-in-law. So, as planned, we married on the twenty second, I in my uniform, and so

were my best man and friends. Food and clothes rationing were still in force, so we had to scrounge coupons from relatives.

The wedding took place at the Methodist Church in Old Hill that we had attended for many years. The reception was held in the adjoining Sunday School room. It was difficult to get a photographer so quickly after the war. The ones we knew were still in the forces. We did get a semi-professional who was quite eager to do the photo's. He took many photo's in and outside the church, but afterwards he disappeared unnoticed when we moved into the reception room. Whilst everyone was seated, and engrossed in the proceedings, up popped a face at a very high window. It was the photographer who had been locked out. He was frantically waving and indicating to be let in. Someone let the frustrated man in to continue taking photo's, after receiving our apologies. The black and white photo's of the wedding turned out to be dark, dull and most disappointing, but it couldn't be helped. We had no honeymoon, but what did I care? All I wanted was to be with my wife and family. Travelling anywhere again was farthest from my mind. We decided to live together at Mary's home with her Aunt Lil, where we stayed for twelve years. In three days it was Christmas, which was another great celebration, the one I had waited for: the first Christmas with my family for six years. In the New Year, my thoughts turned to my future and what employment I should seek. The army pay allowed me time to think, but I had to make an effort. To adjust back to civilian life was not easy, and being married I had a responsibility. I paid a visit to my old employers to meet some of my old workmates. I was told that at least one had been killed. There were changes there: as well as the joinery shop, there was a motor body shop. I wasn't sure if it was what I wanted to do.

Very soon in the year, a letter came offering a place at a rehabilitation centre for service men in the armed forces, to go for interviews to help us find our future employment with the appropriate course of study. The centre was near to Coventry so that meant staying at the centre during the week, and going home weekends. Although it was a wrench to live away from home again, I decided it was worth a try and went. The interviews and talks

amended Ex P.O.W. Course at C.R.U.
9388.   Army Form X 202/B.

CERTIFICATE OF TRANSFER to the ARMY RESERVE

Army No. ...... 5830476 ...... Rank ...... *Pte* ......

Surname (Block letters) ...... *JENNINGS* ......

Christian Name(s) ...... *Jack* ......

Regt. or Corps ...... *Cambs* ......

The transfer of the above-named to the appropriate Class of the Army

Reserve (see note below) is confirmed with effect from — *19. 4. 46.* —

*The date to be inserted here will be that following the day on which Release Leave terminates, including any additional leave to which the soldier may be entitled by virtue of service overseas.

Note.—The appropriate Class of the Army Reserve is as follows :—

(i) Royal Army Reserve—in the case of a regular soldier with reserve service to complete :

(ii) Army Reserve, Class Z (T)—in the case of a man of the Territorial Army, including those called up for service under the National Service Acts :

(iii) Army Reserve, Class Z—in the case of all other soldiers not included in (i) or (ii) above.

Record Office Stamp.

RECORD OFFICE WARWICK

...... *[signature]* Cap.

Officer i/c ...... *Infantry* Records.

Date ...... *8 2 46*.

Warning.—

Any alteration of the particulars given in this certificate may render the holder liable to prosecution under the Seamen's and Soldiers' False Characters Act, 1906.

If this certificate is lost or mislaid, no duplicate can be obtained.

Wt. 45088/4735 1000M 2/45 KJL/7396/16 Gp. 38/3.

Release Leave Certificate, various dates: December 1945 to February 1946

followed. I told them what I would like to do, which was to become a teacher in woodwork. I carried on with that in mind for a while, coming home at weekends. My age then was almost twenty eight, so the thought crossed my mind that if I had to go to college for another few years I would be over thirty before I could settle. The thought of being away from Mary again dampened my spirits, so I left. I felt sure I could get my old job back again. At the first opportunity, I paid a visit to the old firm, where the foreman in the new body shop said he would like me to work for him. I saw the employer who was pleased to see me and have me working for him again. It was arranged for me to start after I was demobbed. Mary was working, so we could manage, with my pay from the army as well.

I had never had six months so easy before in my life. I was able to relax and get back to fitness, doing a few jobs around the house and gardening. Home cooking was suiting me fine, when only a few months before it was dreadful maggoty rice and colourless, vegetable boiled water.

MINISTRY OF PENSIONS

RIGHT OF APPEAL TO TRIBUNAL CONSTITUTED UNDER THE PENSIONS APPEAL TRIBUNALS ACT, 1943.

You will see from the Notice of the Minister's decision set out over-leaf in the form required by the Pensions Appeal Tribunals Act, 1943, that you have the right to appeal to a Tribunal constituted under the Act on the following issues, namely :—

(i) whether the circumstances of your case permit a final settlement of the question to what extent you are disabled ;

(ii) whether the final assessment of the degree or nature of your disablement was right.

On any such appeal the Tribunal may set aside the final assessment on the ground that the circumstances of the case do not permit a final settlement, or may uphold that assessment ; or may make such final assessment of the degree or nature of the disablement as they think proper, which may be either higher or lower than the Minister's assessment.

If you decide to appeal on these issues you must apply to the Ministry of Pensions, Cheltenham, Glos., **not later than** _23rd April 1948_ for a form of Notice of Appeal. PLEASE WRITE AT THE TOP OF ANY LETTER OF APPLICATION THE WORDS "ASSESSMENT APPEAL" and the following reference number _M6/51957_

I met up with some old army friends and they were settling down too. My Best Man at my wedding had made plans to build his own house. We were the lucky ones; other friends fought to survive and died, some with disease, others through lack of strength of mind or body. The most pressing thought on my mind was to get demobbed and start back to work.

The instruction for my demob came for me to go to a depot in Hereford. My sister Iris was a chauffeur for her employer, she told him that I had to go to Hereford for my demob and he gave her permission to use the work's car to take me, so I would have no problem getting there.

With my sister driving, my wife Mary and I were able to enjoy the ride in the country on a lovely spring day. I was one of many there that day to get demobbed, but it didn't take too long. The officer found my record and made out the certificate to say that from that day: the nineteenth of April 1946, I was transferred to Army Reserve Class Z(T), which meant I was a civilian again unless another emergency arose. All my army clothes and kit were handed in, and then I was fitted with a blue striped demob suit. I emerged like a man leaving jail, a happy man to a happy wife and sister.

The return journey was marred when quite suddenly, just as we thought the car ride was perfect, the car spluttered and came to a halt. It wouldn't restart; the petrol gauge told us we were out of petrol. Quite undignified, I in my brand new demob suit, and Mary, had to push the car to a nearby garage for petrol. The car was no further trouble as we continued back home safely. Unknown to my sister at that time, there had been a reserve tank of petrol, which only needed a switch to be moved to *on*, to enable us to reach home trouble free. The hidden switch was disclosed to my sister when she told her employer about the misfortune, much to her embarrassment.

After Whitsuntide I commenced work. The job was to machine assemble, fit and cover wooden framing to complete a mobile ice-cream van, from a drawing. The end product was different from my former work because it involved working with metal fittings and aluminium panels. I worked with the foreman, a former work-mate, doing these purpose-made van and lorry bodies, which I found interesting. Later on as the business developed, we had a long contract to do cabs and bodies, and mount and finish them on their chassis, for Guy Motors. The work was divided into sections, with two to a section, the job progressing to a finish on a piece work rate. The main thing was that I was happy at work and at home.

My mother had found happiness too, besides having me back home she had found a partner, a widower with whom she formed a close relationship. He was a very keen gardener, and helped my mother in the garden and around the house. He and I were like a real father and son very soon. I found him very kind and considerate to my mother and my sisters. In the winter nights we met at weekends often to play cards together. Whenever I went to my mothers in the summer, I was given lettuce, beetroot, in fact anything I wanted that was growing in the large garden.

It was not very surprising when my mother said that she and Arthur were going to be married. So it happened, just over six months after my wedding, my mother tied the knot, with another celebration. We were so pleased for her to find such happiness, after the hard life she had lived, and all the worry throughout the war years, and before.

In the summer of 1946, Mary, my sister Iris and I, with six of the family went on holiday together to Aberystwyth. The meals, which we thought must have come out of tins, were terrible. We complained but it didn't make much difference, though we were aware that food rationing was still in force. Otherwise it was a special holiday in my memory, as it was the first holiday after the end of the war. No-one in the family had a car then, indeed not many families did have one, so we all travelled by train. It was a most picturesque journey through the countryside of Wales, as the stream train slowly weaved its way from station to station.

We had lots of fun together on the beach in beautiful sunny weather. One day we went to Borth beach, and while we were enjoying ourselves, splashing about in the sea in our costumes we were attracted to an unforgettable sight. Mary had moved away to where a youth was propelling himself along on a rubber dinghy. Apparently, he asked her if she would like to try it. She needed no encouragement, and quickly accepted the challenge. As she attempted to scramble aboard, a big wave rolled in to up-end the dinghy and somersault Mary. I knew she couldn't swim, so for a few anxious moments I watched to see Mary surface, laughing happily, having enjoyed the thrill of the somersault. I was quite relieved to see no harm was done.

To finish off the year of celebrations of my homecoming, a small coach load of family and friends spent Christmas at Blackpool. We took our own cases of drinks with us to ensure a wonderful time, although my intake of alcoholic drinks was, and still is, very little.

By this time I had settled down well to the totally different lifestyle of the previous few years. Time had been an important factor in the process of slow healing of mind and body. Another ingredient was keeping busy and enjoying my work, both at my job and at home. I turned my hand to many trades for the first time in my life. Besides woodwork, I interested myself in electrical jobs, painting and decorating, clock repairs, in fact anything to improve the home. It was also the start of me becoming a keen gardener. With the help of books from the local library and magazines, my general knowledge improved, and so did my happiness.

I felt fitter again, thanks to the other ingredient in the rebuilding process, and the most important: the love and attention from my wonderful wife, who cooked good nourishing meals. My gratitude also goes to the help and kindness of her Aunt Lil, with whom we lived so happily together. She was as good as a mother to me.

In the spring of 1947, we were thrilled to get confirmation that our first baby was on the way. On September the fourth, a baby girl added to the happy family. Born at home, we named her Hazel.

Our second baby was born unbelievably on Christmas Day 1948, in a nearby nursing home. We chose Carol to be an appropriate name.

They both grew up together and attended the same schools, and as a family we went out often at weekends on picnics in the countryside, especially when we had our first car in 1952. Their childhood seemed to pass so quickly, with lots of happy memories at home and on holidays.

They made us very proud parents when they studied well and both went to college to become teachers.

There are lots of stories which could be told of the years following their birth to the present day, but that is another story, which may be told by them one day. I am sure they could make it just as interesting. Who knows what interesting things could take place in the twenty-first century.

Epilogue 1

For many years after returning from the horrible conditions which P.O.Ws in the Far East endured, I, like many of my colleagues, found getting back to normal was not easy. Some had a disability or injury, but everyone had suffered from tropical diseases. Moreover, malnutrition, together with long hard days of slavery, reduced even the youngest of prisoners to poor weaklings. In these dreadful conditions many were made to walk long distances in the hot sun or pouring rain, with the briefest of clothing, over rough terrain, with or without footwear. Many were beaten for not being able to carry on.

The hardship and torture that we received will never be forgotten or forgiven, because in just a few years as a P.O.W. many lost their will to live, and died. They were once fighting fit and proud servicemen. If it had been possible to film the atrocities committed by the Japanese tormentors, and the conditions in which the P.O.W.s lived, it would have been too ghastly to show.

Those of us who returned home from the Far East prisoner of war camps were very lucky indeed. However, many of those suffered ill health and died within a few years. I was one of the lucky survivors, although I had my fair share of bouts of malaria, dysentery, dengue fever (which causes swelling of the joints), renal colic, and a large leg ulcer, as well as the inevitable skin complaints, which were very unpleasant.

I had a long spell working on the railway from Chungkai to Wun Lung, on to Wun Tu Kin, and Bankao, digging and carrying earth to form the embankment. I also helped to construct bridges, which involved cutting down trees, debarking, squaring to form a beam, tapering piles, all with primitive tools. Then pile driving, by pulling a heavy weight to the top of a tripod, releasing quickly, repeating until the pile was sunk low enough. Other times I was in a two man team, cutting down trees, sawing to half-metre lengths and chopping to the size required, and stacked one metre high by the track.

My next move to Rintin camp might have been the one that saved my life. It was a shocking camp, situated a good distance up from Bankao. During the first or second night, I was in severe pain, causing me to cry out, waking others in the hut. The medical officer came to see me next morning and diagnosed appendicitis. Arrangement was made for me to be evacuated back to Chungkai base camp. At Chungkai the medical officer there found that I had Renal Colic, not appendicitis. After recovering from that I had an ulcer on my leg. This kept me at Chungkai until May '44. Many who had ulcers at the same time as me had to have amputations by primitive methods. I firmly believe that the evacuation from Rintin to Chungkai, and the fact that my ulcer healed, saved my life.

Within a few months of returning home and enjoying a happy married life, I began to settle to my new style of living. Occasionally I had bouts of shivering. Sometimes I would have unpleasant dreams and awaken my wife, shouting! I didn't talk about my experiences, and I wasn't pressed to do so.

In 1995 (The 50th Anniversary of the end of the war), I was able to go with my elder daughter, Hazel, on a Pilgrimage to Singapore and Thailand, returning to places where we were during the battle and other interesting places too.

The flimsy structure of the bridge on bamboo stilts against the rock and overhanging the River Kwai Noi.

The famous dangerous stretch of railway at Wam Po built by P.O.W.s during the war - crossing the line 50 years on.

Hazel and myself on the bridge escape section, looking down the River Kwai Noi.

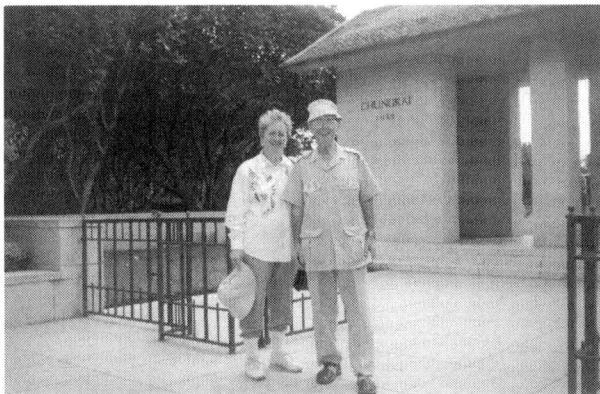

Hazel and me at Chungkai

In Thailand we visited the two cemeteries, Chungkai and Kanchanaburi, and the Bridge on the Kwai. Along with many other experiences, we also had a train trip on the Thai Railway which I helped to build. The memory of the horror of P.O.W. life along the railway that had remained with me for many years faded quickly, as the once thick jungle had gone, so had the camps. Now the scenery is enjoyed by many tourists. I was able to take lots of photos, which I treasure.

Again, in 2005 I was able to return with my younger daughter, Carol, on a similar tour to Singapore and Thailand, but with special invitations and hospitality accorded to honour the fourteen or so veterans in a party of seventy. The highlights were being invited to the High Commissioner's house for evening dinner and another invite to lunch by the President of the Ex-Services Association of Singapore. In Thailand the British Ambassador attended three or four of the places we went to.

On the tour was a Japanese lady who was a Professor at a University in Japan. She was eager to listen to our experiences, and at her request she recorded a three hour interview with me. I have no animosity to her generation at all, in fact a number of years ago a Japanese young man who I met on holiday in Eastbourne, wrote to me asking if we could meet up on his visit to Birmingham. I replied, inviting him to come, with pleasure. We met him at New Street station and brought him back home to have dinner with us.

Comparing stories with a fellow veteran

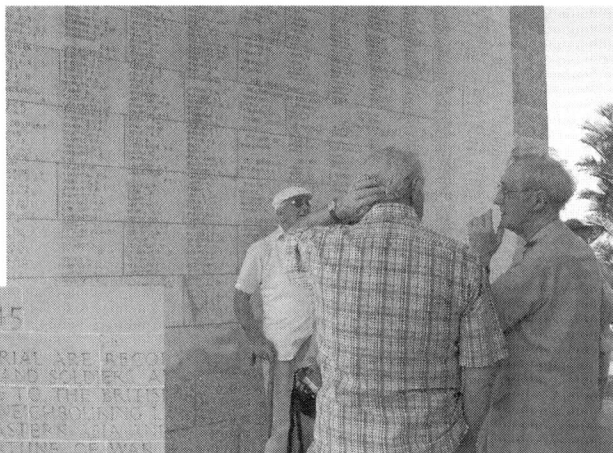

With Carol at Changi Cemetery

Visiting Hellfire Pass

The railway now terminates at Namtok: The remainder of the line to the border was dismantled by the Thailand State Railway – much of its route is now under water.

The Gravestone of Billy Welch at Kanchaniburi. We served together in The Cambridgeshires. On my return from the Pilgrimage in 2005, I had the top picture published in a local paper: *The Black Country Bugle*. As a result I was contacted by his sister and nephew, who had no idea where he was buried. They subsequently planned a pilgrimage of their own.

The modern 'Bridge On The River Kwai', rebuilt by a Japanese company as part of war reparations

My feeling for the Japanese guards who were with us, and all who allowed them to commit such barbaric crimes stays the same. I will never forget or forgive. There were massacres wherever they went over many years. Only recently have their people learned what dreadful acts were committed by their armies, but you cannot blame the people.

Epilogue 2

In 2010 I had another opportunity to return to Singapore and Thailand, this time with my grand-daughter, Carolyn. I was due to travel out on the 5th of November, but when I had the misfortune to fall and break my hip in July of that year the whole trip was put in jeopardy. However, I was determined that I would go on the tour, and with daily exercise and walks to strengthen the muscles, my rehabilitation progressed rapidly. My main concern was standing around at the cemeteries for Remembrance services, so I took a folding walking stick.

During the nine hour flight to Singapore I exercised my legs as much as possible, which enabled me to do all the tours, and much more, without the aid of the stick.

One day in Singapore a newspaper reporter came to the hotel and interviewed the three veterans and a few widows of veterans on the tour. These interviews were reported and printed in the Friday, November 12th Today newspaper, with the photo of me displaying the chess set which I carved with my penknife during the latter period of being a prisoner of the Japanese.

The Singapore television Forces Network also interviewed me, and took many photos. They followed me around Kranji cemetery, taking

photos and recording, as I placed a poppy spray on one of my comrades' grave-stones. They followed me to where a group of school-children and their teacher surrounded me and asked me questions about my wartime experiences in Singapore. This was shown on television as part of a war history programme.

The Changi Museum was well worth another visit. On the walls are copies of the original murals which were painted by a sick POW on the walls of a small room, set up by the prisoners as a chapel, at the end of the dysentery wing of the hospital block. Carolyn took many photographs of biblical scenes: *Nativity, Ascension, Last Supper, Crucifixion* and *Saint Luke.* The originals were done with paint made with a tin of white paint and dyes from billiard chalk and other materials found around the camp. Some brushes were made from human hair.

On the 11th November we departed from Singapore to Bankok and transferred to our hotel.

Next morning we were taken by church to Kanchanaburi and Chungkai cemeteries for personal visits and memorial services. A

remarkable coincidence occurred at Chungkai:

An extract from an article written by David Everett and published in the COFEPOW Newsletter early in 2011, tells the story of the above photographs:

At our very first local COFEPOW meeting in April 2010, our surprise guest of honour was nonagenarian Jack Jennings (father of COFEPOW member Carol Barrett) who had been a Private in the 1st Battalion Cambridgeshire Regiment when Singapore fell to the Japanese.

Over lunch, we talked about my father, Private Stanley Everett of the 5th Battalion Suffolk Regiment, who like Jack had worked on the Burma Railway but died at Chungkai military base hospital in July, 1943.

Mentioning that he was returning to Singapore in November to attend a Memorial Service, Jack kindly offered to take some photographs of Dad's grave in Chungkai military cemetery. Fortunately, I had exact details of where his grave was located and true to his word, I received four wonderful pictures the day before my 69th birthday in November.

There is however, a story that goes with these photographs.

As Jack was about to take them, the camera's battery unfortunately gave up the ghost. Just as this happened, he looked up to see two familiar figures walking in his direction, COFEPOW members Glynn and Judith Cocker from Doncaster, whom he had met on a visit to a 'COFEPOW North' meeting in Manchester.

Glynn volunteered to take the photographs with his own camera and did a fine job. Prior to visiting Dad's grave, Jack had very kindly bought a wreath and written a special message on our behalf and these, along with Jack, feature in Glynn's photographs. It was good to know that the original plain cross with simple lettering erected after the war had long since been replaced with such a fine and beautifully inscribed gravestone. I wish my Mum could have lived to see these pictures.

They certainly were one of the best birthday presents I could have had. I felt that Dad really had an old friend standing next to him that day. Glynn's excellent photography and Jack's thoughtful gestures really did Dad proud.

At our pre-Christmas COFEPOW meeting in December, we then had the pleasure of meeting Glynn and Judith Cocker (just back from Singapore) and thanking them for being in the right place at the right time! And all this happened as a result of our first meeting.

To conclude, one of the nicest comments we have received so far regarding our meetings came recently from Carol Barrett saying 'how special our meetings are, as though we are part of a family'. Couldn't have put it better myself!

Continuing our tour, in the afternoon we went on the train along the Burma-Siam Death Railway from Kanchanaburi to Namtok.

Afterwards we checked-in at the River Kwai Hotel. From there we went by coach to Hellfire Pass and Museum; a grim reminder of the hard work on the railway.

On Sunday 14th November we were invited to join the British Ambassador in the grounds of the Embassy for their Armistice Service and lunch.

What a pleasure it was to go back again to the Far East and to see the delightful beauty of the very interesting locations in both Singapore and Thailand and to enjoy every tourist attraction. It was such a vivid contrast to the awful scenes that we as prisoners had to witness and endure: the lack of medical supplies to ease pain and suffering; needless deaths from the many tropical diseases that all the prisoners had to endure; enforced work parties whilst suffering from fevers and having very little food.

Epilogue 3

In 2015, Jack made what he expected to be his last return to the Far East. The following recount, written by Paul, was published in the NFFWRA Newsletter.

As the sun set over the Bridge On the River Kwai, three survivors of the horrors inflicted by the Japanese stood overlooking the river whilst some of the millions of annual visitors to this iconic site clamoured to have their pictures taken with them.

Jim Crossan (98), Jack Jennings (96) and Maurice Naylor (94) were the focus of everyone's attention. They were taking part in the FEPOW 70 Years Remembrance Group Tour of Singapore and Thailand, which took place at the end of October, 2015.

The entire party consisted of thirty-six individuals, all of whom had a connection with the events in the region seventy years previously. The group included widows, sons, daughters and, indeed, grandchildren of FEPOWS. There were also historians who took the opportunity to use the knowledge of the FEPOWs to further their research. The trip was organised by Remembrance Travel and ably led by Gerry Norden.

The Pilgrimage had commenced in Singapore. The first full day began with a visit to the causeway and a spot where Maurice recalled standing as he watched the Japanese cross to the island. The CWGC Cemetery on Singapore Island is located not far from the causeway at Kranji and we took the opportunity to visit the site to undertake personal remembrances.

Later in the day we toured the Changi area. The famous Changi Murals are located in a building in the middle of an Air Force Base. We were fortunate to be granted a unique opportunity to view these remarkable paintings (they are replicated at the Changi Gaol Museum) that were produced by Stanley Warren when he was a prisoner of the Japanese.

Our day ended with a visit to the Museum at Changi Gaol and our

first experience, repeated endlessly throughout the rest of the trip, of complete strangers approaching 'our' veterans wishing to hear about their wartime experiences.

Wednesday morning saw us return to Kranji for a Service of Remembrance. We were joined by the Year 9 history class from Dulwich College. FEPOW Chaplain Pauline Simpson led the service which included readings of poetry and the address made by an army chaplain at the first service after the Japanese surrendered. The service concluded with laying of wreaths.

The Battle Box in Canning Park was the location of the Allied Headquarters during the Japanese Invasion. The HQ has been reconstructed using waxwork models in order to retell the story of the Fall of Singapore. It has been closed for a couple of years for refurbishment but we were granted special permission to visit the site.

Following a buffet lunch at Dulwich College, the pupils were given an opportunity to participate in a question and answer session with the veterans. Their great sense of humour which enabled them to survive the war was obvious in the answers they gave to the thoughtful questions.

We returned to our hotel via Alexandra Hospital, scene of the most notorious atrocities of the invasion. That evening we were invited to the Military Attaché's residence for a fish supper.

The Old Ford Factory was the location of our first visit the following day. On 15th February 1942 the Allied High Command travelled from the Battle Box to the factory in order to negotiate the terms of the Allied surrender. Following our visits to these two locations, many of our party felt a great deal of sympathy for LG Percival. He was a man not suited to his role, surrounded by a group of senior officers who all seemed to hate each other.

Lunch was taken at The British Club, after which Jon Cooper, a battlefield archaeologist, outlined the work he had undertaken at Adam Park – the location of the 1st Cambridgeshire Battalion at the time of the surrender. Over the previous six years, he and his team had undertaken a series of digs in the area in order to establish the order of events at the location. The Park was also the location of a POW camp and Jon had recently found evidence of a Chapel in one of the houses.

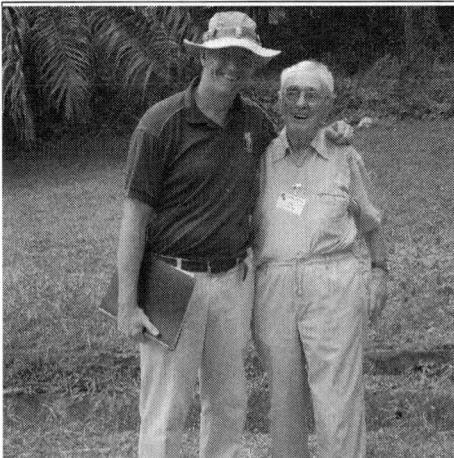

Jack with Jon Cooper, in front of the newly rediscovered trench

The afternoon was spent touring Adam Park. Jack, a veteran of the 1st Cambridgeshires, expressed surprise at how little the location had changed in the past seventy-five years. One thing that had puzzled Jon over the years was the location of the slit trench in front of BHQ. To Jon's delight, Jack was able to pinpoint the trench as being alongside an overgrown hedge on the edge of the estate.

Most members of the pilgrimage took the opportunity to relax on Saturday, our designated 'free day'. It was fortunate that nothing was planned for this day because the pollution levels were officially 'hazardous'.

Sunday was transfer day, when we travelled from Singapore to Kanchanaburi - a considerable improvement on the journey experienced by our veterans over seventy years previously. As night was falling, we stopped briefly outside the school playing field that was the location of the Ban Pong Camp where all the prisoners from Singapore passed through on the way to the Death Railway. The Ban Pong Station is still operational, another stop allowed us to see it in action.

On Monday, we visited the Thailand-Burma Railway Centre (TBRC) to meet our hosts for the week, amongst whom was Rod Beattie, the world's leading authority on the Death Railway. Two out of the three CWGC Cemeteries on the railway are located in the area around Kanchanaburi and our next appointments were Remembrance Services at each of them.

The main service took place at the cemetery in the town. Rod Beattie introduced the service which was then led by

119

Pauline. The service included readings and poetry as well as The Last Post, Reveille and prayers. It was followed by a wreath laying ceremony. A large number of wreaths were carried to the Cross of Sacrifice, each wreath being placed on behalf of a regiment or organisation connected to our pilgrimage.

The other cemetery is a few miles down the line at Chungkai. The ceremony was briefer here but included a moving reminiscence from Maurice about a former colleague of his who is buried in the cemetery.

Jack reading the FEPOW Prayer
(with Pauline Simpson)

Being interviewed by John Irvine

Throughout the day, we were being filmed by John Irvine and an ITV News cameraman. Part of the report that appeared on the evening's news bulletins focussed on Jim's pilgrimage to an old pal's grave and featured him singing 'Abide With Me' at the graveside.

Lunch at a floating restaurant was followed by the obligatory visit to 'The Bridge'. The film crew stayed with us, promoting the scenes of curious tourists wanting to get their 'selfie' with Jim, Jack and Maurice.

Jack and Paul

The following two days saw us travelling 'up-country', following the route of the railway as far as the Myanmar border at the Three Pagodas Pass. Beyond Nam Tok the railway no longer exists but we tried to follow its route as closely as possible – this resulted in us occasionally getting tangled up in overhanging trees on some of the narrow back roads. We stopped at a number of POW sites along the way, paying particular attention to sites where family members of our pilgrims had been. Although some of these places contain memorials to the Death Railway we were pleased to see that many of them have 'moved on' and become quite attractive tourist resorts.

We spent the night on a resort overlooking the lake that now covers part of the railway before shopping briefly in the Songkurai area. This was the most notorious stretch of the line, with a higher percentage of deaths than anywhere else during the construction. The reputation of the British officers at this site was very low and, indeed, it was events at this POW camp on which Pierre Boulle based his book, The Bridge On the River Kwai.

After a break at the Thee Pagodas Pass we headed back south. The afternoon was spent at Hellfire Pass. This location has taken on iconic status and has become the focus of Australian FEPOW Memorial events. After visiting the somewhat disappointing museum, many of the pilgrims walked down to the pass. The heat and humidity, even during this short exertion, gave one a greater appreciation of the hardships that the FEPOWs went through during the war – and we were only walking!

The day ended with us watching the sun set over Ban Pong viaduct.

Thursday came and at last we got to ride on the railway. Setting off from Kanchanaburi, we crossed 'the Bridge' before continuing on as far as the Ban Pong viaduct. A meal at a restaurant overlooking the river was followed by a coach journey back to our resort. Most of our party chose to spend the afternoon relaxing by the pool.

Friday morning saw a return to Kanchanaburi where FEPOWs and their families took the opportunity to undertake personal research at the TBRC. The resources and knowledge available at the centre are

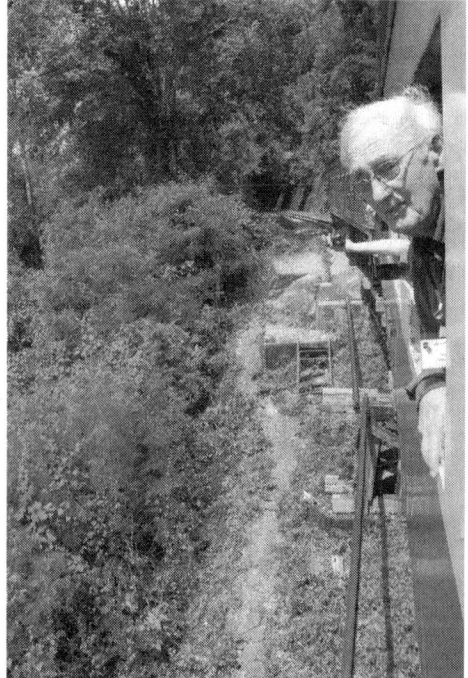

remarkable.

Everyone enjoyed the gala dinner that evening, some of us taking the opportunity to get quite adventurous with the local cuisine. Speeches and presentations were made and we were able to express our appreciation to Rod and his team for the wonderful way they had looked after and helped us throughout the week.

Bangkok was our destination on the final morning. We visited Christ Church (aka the FEPOW Church) in the city and were treated to a buffet lunch. The parish priest explained the history of the church in Thailand but was unable to explain why it was known as the FEPOW Church, beyond the fact that the handles on one of the doors contained the FEPOW emblem.

Our final port of call before our long flight home was the British Embassy where we were treated to high tea by the Ambassador and his wife. The three FEPOWs took pride of place in the visitors' book.

It was a busy and, at times, very tiring and emotional two weeks. There were times of sadness, particularly during the visits to the cemeteries, but also of great joy.

For many of us, it was a once in a lifetime experience and the opportunity to spend time in the company of railway veterans is one we will never forget. Some of us resolved to return to Singapore and Thailand with future generations of our families in order to keep the story alive. Their sacrifice should never be allowed to be forgotten.

APPENDICES

Appendix 1: Far East Campaign Japanese Invasion of Malaya

Appendix 2: Where the dead of the Thai-Burma Railroad are buried

Appendix 3: Major Prison Camps

Appendix 4: Railway map

Appendix 5: Medical Discharge Certificates

Appendix 6: Japanese Index Card

Appendix 7: POW Questionnaire and Major David Nelson's Diary

Appendix 8: Timeline

Appendix 1

Malayan Singapore Campaign

Official figures show Allied losses during the Malayan Campaign amounted to 138,108. These included 38,496 British, 18,490 Australian, 61,340 Indian and 14,382 local volunteers. Over 130,000 of these were captured - mainly in Singapore.

Far East Campaign Against Japanese

The Japanese took about 9,000 New Zealand prisoners during The Second World War in the Far East. In their official history books, the recounting of their story takes up a whole volume. The Australians with about 22,000 prisoners recounted their story in official history in 110 pages; but the British with about 136,000 prisoners of the Japanese could only fill 10 pages in five volumes of The War Against Japan. *That is a disgraceful and disrespectful account of the prisoners' sacrifice in inhumane conditions. Their experiences covered nearly four years of the war and were remarkable, truly amazing and a credit to their country.*

The construction of the infamous Thailand to Burma railway began when the first POWs were taken from Singapore by train to Nong Pladuk in Thailand in the month of June 1942. After first constructing primitive shelters for living and cooking, then cover for work tools, work got under way to construct the railway up to the Burma border, a distance of 263kms. Other POWs taken mainly from Sumatra and Java were later to begin constructing the railway to join the existing station to the Moulmein- Ye line at Thanbyuzayat, working south towards the Thailand border to join up with the Thailand workforce. Under Japanese railway engineers' supervision the POW workers were selected into parties according to their trade or skills.

The Japanese soldiers, as guards, took orders from the engineers to enforce the daily tasks set. Work at first entailed clearing the jungle of trees or bamboo where the railroad was marked out. The embankment where

126

required was marked with profiles to show the exact ground level, rake and height. Parties of workers were split into small groups to collect, carry and dump earth to conform to the profiles. At first the embankment was low, but in places it rose up to as much as 15-20 feet. Each few feet were consolidated by all parties walking up and down.

Bridges large and small were constructed with newly hewn timber and bamboo on the spot. The prisoners blasted through rock formations to form cuttings.

The Thailand workforce constructed 263 km of track of the 415km long Burma-Thailand Railway. According to Japanese estimates the building of the railway involved digging carrying and dumping 4,000,000 cubic metres of earth; drilling for blasting and moving 3,000,000 cubic metres of rock; constructing 14 km of bridgework; using 60,000 cubic feet of timber and 650,000 cubic feet of poles. The blasting of rock to form cuttings used 300 tons of explosives. Several hundred lorries and motor boats were used to carry materials and 400 elephants to work moving trees. Prisoners moved many trees into place when the elephants refused.

There were 688 bridges constructed on the railway, all except 8 were wooden.

By May 1943 major obstacles at Tamarkan Chungkai and Wampo were overcome and the railway was operational as far as Tarsao, 130 km from Nong Plad Duk.

On 22nd May 1943 the monsoon broke the bridge at Hintok which was 1/4 of a mile long and 80 feet high. The track was finished and joined with ceremony on 17th October 1943.

Appendix 2

Where the dead of the Thailand-Burma Railway lie buried

Country of Origin	Total POWs/ Labourers#	CHUNGKAI	KANCHANABURI
British	30,131	1,384	3,568
Dutch	17,990	313	1,896
Australian	13,004	-	1,362
Malayan	≈ 75,000	37	104
Indian		6	12
N. Zealand		-	2
Canadian		-	1
Burmese	≈ 90,000	-	1
Unknown		-	35
American	686	-	-
Other		-	1
Aminese	200		
Chinese (Singapore)	5,200		
Javanese	7,500		
SUBTOTAL	≈ 240,000	1,740	6,982*
Japanese/ Korean	15,000		
TOTAL	≈ 255,000		

*This figure includes 300 men who died of cholera and were cremated. Their ashes are buried in two graves in the cemetery and their names inscribed on panels in the shelter pavilion.

#These figures courtesy of work carried out by researchers at TBRC.

At the end of the war, there were 10,549 graves (in 144 cemeteries) recorded on or near the railway. Only 52 of these were not found in post-war search and relocation of these graves.

Country of Origin	THANBYUZAYAT	Total	Total Deaths#	%#
British	1,588	6,540	6,648	22%
Dutch	621	2,830	2,830	16%
Australian	1,348	2,710	2,710	21%
Malayan	79	220	≈42,000	56%
Indian	15	33	33	
N. Zealand	3	5	5	
Canadian	1	2	2	
Burmese	1	2	≈40,000	44%
Unknown	114	149		
American	-	remains repatriated	132	19%
Other	1	2	2	
Aminese			25	13%
Chinese (Singapore)			500	10%
Javanese			2,900	39%
	3,771	**12,493**	**≈98,000**	
Japanese/ Korean			≈ 1,000	7%
			≈ 99,000	

A small number of POWs who died did not receive the formality of having a known grave in one of the three war cemeteries. There are a number of reasons for this:

- Some men drowned in the river or attempted to escape and their bodies could not be recovered;
- In some camps a number of bodies were cremated on large communal cremation pyres;
- Those who died in transit were buried in roadside graves;
- Burial records were sometimes lost.

These individuals are commemorated on the Singapore Memorial.

Appendix 3

Major Prison camps built on the side of the railway

The Japanese used local place names during the building and operation of the railway. Spellings of the camp names varies from source to source, mainly due to the Asian pronunciation of the letters *l* and *r* and the different languages and dialects spoken on the railway. Many of the stations have the same name as the construction camps. Although they were built later, stations were often built in the same location because the physical conditions that suit a camp are the same as the requirements for a station – a large area of flat level ground and a water supply.

The following list is based upon work undertaken by Rod Beattie. Almost all of the camps in Burma were known by the distance the camps were from Thanbyuzayat.

(Including approximate railway distances in km from Nong Pladuk)

The camps that Jack recalls in his memoirs are highlighted in **bold**.

Camps	Km	Stations
Nakhon Pathom		
(Hospital camp)		
Nong Pladuk (2 camps)	0.00	Nong Pladuk
	2.00	Khok Mo
[1]**Ban Pong Junction**	3.30	
(Start of Railway)		
	5.18	Bang Pong Mai
	13.38	Ruk Khe
Tha Rua	25.89	Tha Rua Noi
Tha Muang	38.90	Tha Muang
	43.00	Khao Din Railway Workshops
[2]**Kanchanaburi Hospital 2**	49.60	
	50.32	Kanchanaburi
Aerodrome Nos. 1 & 2	51.20	
Kanchanaburi Hospital 1	52.00	
[3]Tha Makham (Tamarkan)	56.20	

(Bridge on the River Kwai)

130

	57.30	Khao Poon
[4]Chungkai	60.00	
Wang Lan	68.59	Wang Lan
Wang Yen	74.40	
	77.66	Tha Pong
Wang Takhian	81.30	
Ban Khao	87.93	Ban Khao
Tha Kilen	97.89	Tha Kilen
Nong Pradai	101.60	
	108.14	Ai Hit
Arrow Hill	109.80	
Wang Pho South	111.50	

[5](Wang Pho viaducts)

Wang Pho Central	112.10	
	114.04	Wang Pho
Wang Pho North	115.80	
Pukai	118.60	
Wang Yai	124.85	Wang Yai
[6]Tha Sao Hospital	125.00	
Tha Soa North	125.00	

(Nam Tok – end of operating line)

	130.30	Tha Sao
Tonchan South	131.50	
Tonchan Bridge	132.70	
Tonchan Central	138.80	
	139.05	Tonchan
Tonchan Spring	140.30	
Tampii South	144.00	
Tampii	147.52	Tampii
Kannyu South	149.50	
Lower Kannyu (2 camps)	151.00	
Upper Kannyu	151.00	
[7]Kannyu No. 3	152.50	

(Hellfire Pass)

Malay Hamlet	153.00	
Hin Tok Road (2 camps)	154.00	
	155.03	Hin Tok

Hin Tok River (2 camps)	156.00	
Hin Tok Cement	157.00	
Kinsaiyok Jungle No.1	161.40	Kannyu
Kinsaiyok Jungle No.2	167.70	Saiyok
Kinsaiyok Main	170.20	
	171.72	Kinsaiyok
Bhatona	173.70	
	180.53	Lin Thin
Lin Thin (Rin Tin)	182.00	
Kui Yae	185.60	
	190.48	Kui Yae
Kuishi	190.50	
Wang Hin	191.70	
Hindat West	197.20	
Hindat	197.75	Hindat
Kui Mang	198.70	
Linson (3 camps)	202.50	
Prang Kasi South	207.00	
Prang Kasi	208.11	Prang Kasi
Prang Kasi (211 Kilo)	211.00	
Ongthi	213.20	
	213.80	Ongthi
Bangan	214.60	
Tha Khanun South	217.70	
	218.15	Tha Khanun
Tha Khanun (Australian)	222.40	
Tha Khanun Base	223.40	
Tha Khanun North	225.00	
Nam Chon Yai	229.14	Nam Chon Yai
Tha Mayo	236.80	Tha Mayo
Tha Mayo Wood	239.00	
Johnson's Camp	244.19	Tamrong Phatho
Dobb's Camp	246.00	
Swinton's Camp	249.00	
Kroeng Krai	250.13	Kroeng Krai
Konkoita 'H' Force No. 2	252.90	
Kurikonta	257.70	
Konkoita	262.53	Konkoita

⁸(Joining Point 262.87)

Lower Thimongtha	269.80	
Thimongtha	271.80	
	273.06	Thimongtha
Shimon Ni Thea	276.00	Shimon Ni Thea
Ni Thea Bridge Building	280.50	
⁹Ni Thea	281.80	Ni Thea
131 Kilo (Little Ni Thea)	284.10	
Shimo Sonkurai	288.10	
122 Kilo	293.00	
Songkurai	294.02	Songkurai
116 Kilo	299.00	
Kami Sonkurai	299.20	
Chaunggahla-ya	300.90	
	303.95	Chaunggahla-ya

¹⁰(Three Pagodas border crossing)

108 Kilo	306.90	Paya-thonzu Taung
105 Kilo	310.63	Aungganaung
100 Kilo	315.00	Regue
98 Kilo	317.00	
95 Kilo (Kyondaw)	319.88	Kyondaw
90 Kilo (Tadein)	321.10	
85 Kilo (Lawa)	325.30	
	332.09	Apalon
82 Kilo (Apalon)	332.60	
80 Kilo (Apalaine)	337.25	Apalaine
75 Kilo(Meiloe)	340.00	
	342.83	Mezali
70 Kilo (Mezali)	346.00	
	348.66	Kami Mezali
65 Kilo (Kami Mezali)	350.00	
	353.77	Lonsi
62 Kilo (Lonsi)	354.00	
60 Kilo (Taungzun)	355.00	
	357.60	Taungzun
55 Kilo Hospital	360.00	
	361.90	ThanbayaThanbaya

		Hospital
Thanbaya Hospital	365.00	
	366.06	Anankwin
45 Kilo (Anankwin)	370.00	
40 Kilo (Beketaung)	374.20	
	374.40	Beketaung
35 Kilo (Tanyin)	379.92	Tanyin
30 Kilo (Retphaw)	384.59	Retphaw
26 Kilo (Kunhnitkway))	391.02	Konnoi
18 Kilo (Hlepauk)	396.39	Rabao
14 Kilo (Thetkaw)	401.34	Thetkaw
8 Kilo (Wagale)	406.10	
	406.37	Wagale
4 Kilo (Kandaw)	409.79	Sin-Thanbyuzayat
11 Thanbyuzayat	414.60	
	414.92	Thanbyuzayat

Footnotes to POW Camps

1. Ban Pong was the arrival point for POWs sent to Thailand from Singapore. 28 men were crammed into steel railway box-cars for the five day trip.
2. Kanchanaburi was the site of the Japanese Headquarters for the railway construction in Thailand. Construction of the southern part of the railway was supervised by the Japanese 9th Railway Regiment.
3. Tha Makham is the site of the 'Bridge on the River Kwai'.
4. Chungkai was the site of a large hospital camp. The War Cemetery at Chungkai is the cemetery established by the POWs in 1943. The first burial in the cemetery is Grave 7.G.1.
5. Wang Pho is famous as the site of the large wooden viaduct built into a cliff face by British POWs.
6. Tha Sao was the site of another large hospital camp. The thousands of men who died here are now buried in Kanchanaburi War Cemetery.
7. Kannyu No. 3 and Malay hamlet housed many of the men who worked on 'Hellfire Pass'.
8. Konkoita is the place where the groups constructing the railway from the south met the groups working from the north on 16th October 1943. This area is now flooded following the building of the Vachiralongkorn Dam in 1985.
9. Ni Thea was the headquarters for the ill-fated 'F' Force. This group of 7,000 British and Australian POWs suffered more than 3,000 deaths in eight months from May to December 1943.
10. Three Pagodas mark the border crossing between Burma and Thailand. This area was the scene of an ancient battle between the two countries. The three small pagodas were built to commemorate this battle.
11. Thanbyuzayat was the base camp for the railway construction groups on Burma. The Japanese 5th Railway Regiment was headquartered here. The war cemetery at Thanbyuzayat is the original cemetery established by the POWs.

APPENDIX 4 # The Thai-Burn

June 1942 - Octo

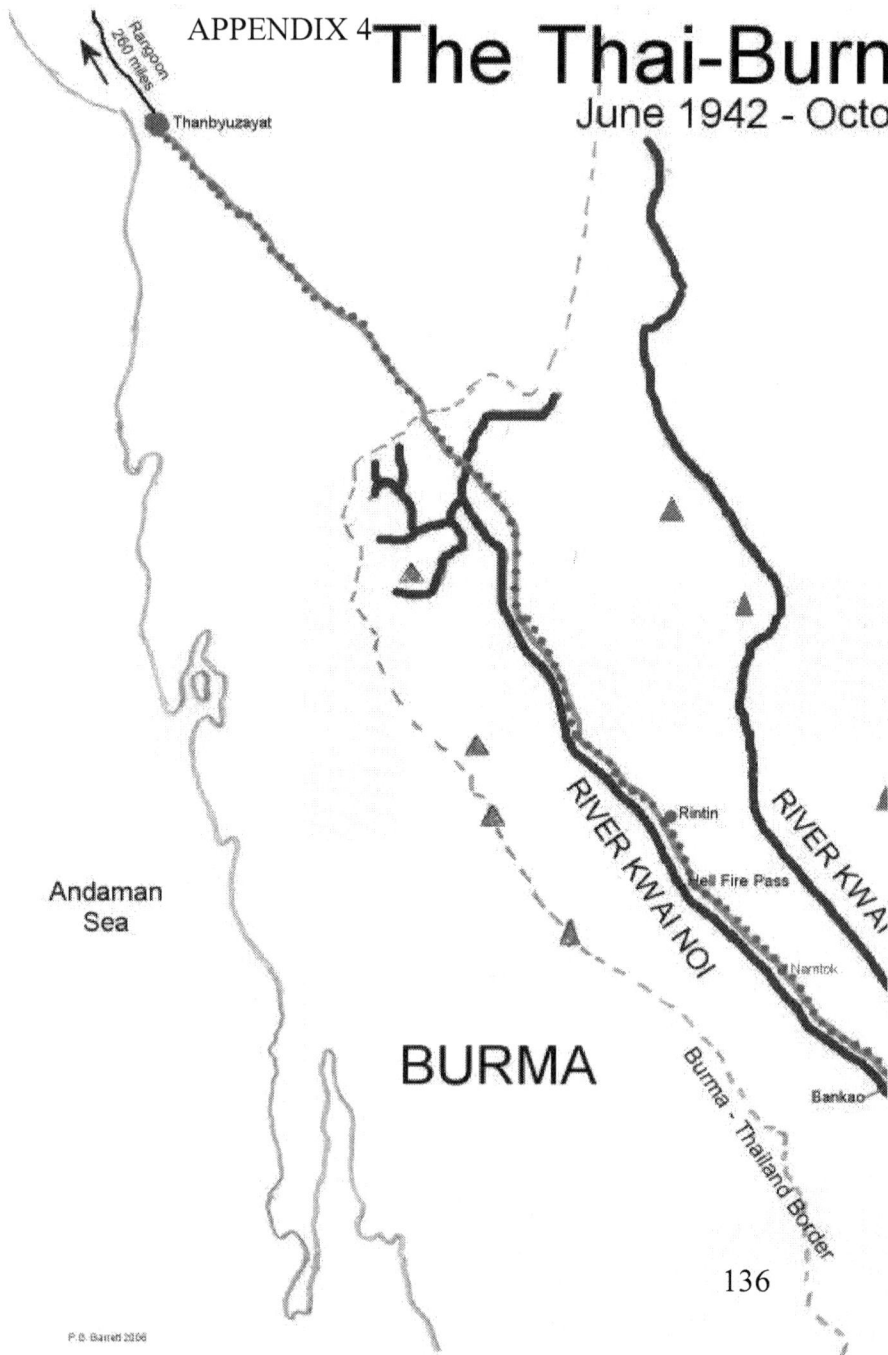

Rangoon 260 miles

Thanbyuzayat

Andaman Sea

RIVER KWAI NOI

RIVER KWAI

Rintin

Hell Fire Pass

Namtok

Bankao

BURMA

Burma - Thailand Border

136

P.B. Barrett 2006

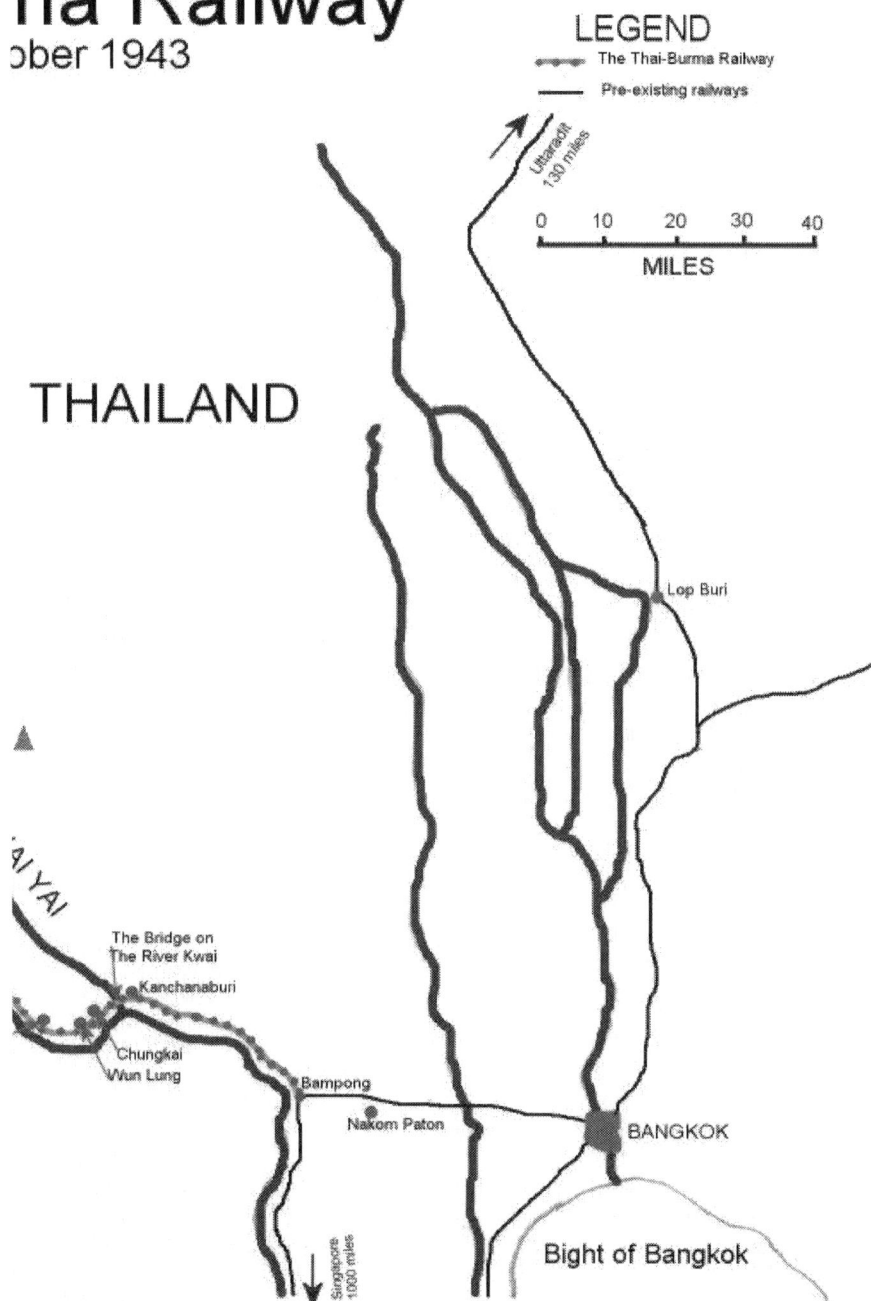

na Railway
ober 1943

Uttaradit
130 miles

0   10   20   30   40
MILES

THAILAND

Lop Buri

AI YAI

The Bridge on
The River Kwai

Kanchanaburi

Chungkai
Wun Lung

Bampong

Nakom Paton

BANGKOK

Singapore
1000 miles

Bight of Bangkok

137

Appendix 5
Medical Discharge Certificates

These two small slips of paper contain details of my medical record, admittance and discharge dates; also the treatments in brief. It just shows that even in the restricted and harsh conditions in which the POW camp doctors worked they developed a system to keep records.

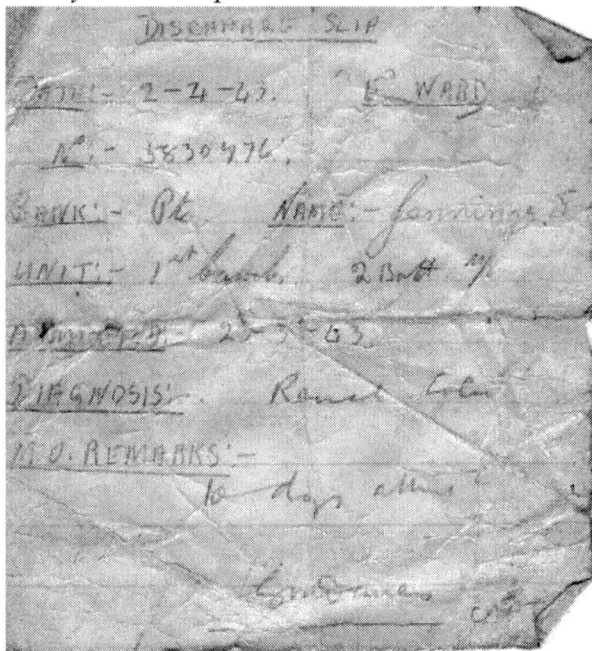

DISCHARGE SLIP

DATE:- 2-4-43 'E' WARD
  N°:- 5830776
RANK:- Pte   NAME:- Jennings J
UNIT:- 1st Camb.   2 Batt
ADMITTED:- 23-3-43
DIAGNOSIS:- Renal Colic
M.O. REMARKS:-
              10 days attend sp
              G M Davies   *CAPT*

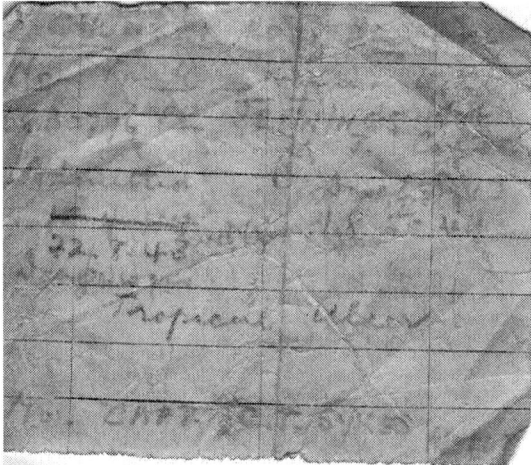

CHUNKAI HOSPITAL CAMP

No	Rank	Name
5830776	Pte	Jennings J.

Admitted	Discharged
22 – 8 – 43	18 – 5 – 44

Diagnosis
    Tropical Ulcer

M.O. CAPT. J.C.T. SYKES R.A.M.C.

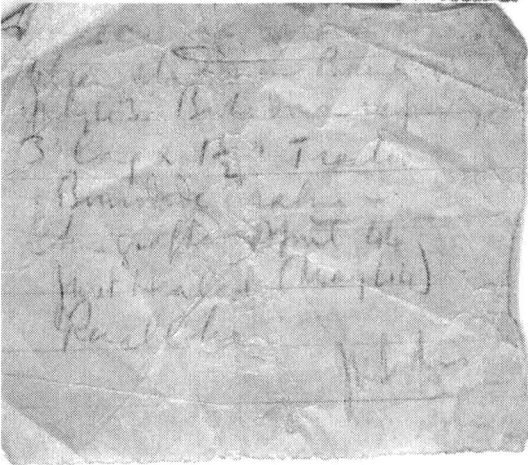

RECORD OF CASE HISTORY

Ulcer started with bamboo scratch
July '43
3" long x 1½ Treatment
    Binidide   Saline
Skin grafted April 44
Just Healed May 44
Renal Colic

J.C.T. SYKES

Appendix 6
Japanese Index Card

At the end of the war, the War Office took into their possession 50,000 index cards which the Japanese compiled. The personal details are in English, but the other information is in Japanese. Copies of these cards are now available from the National Archives (Ref. WO345).

In the box headed **Camp:** The characters indicate *Malaya Prisoner of War Camp*. They are crossed through, indicating a transfer – this is confirmed by the character above which is *Thailand*.

No.: Almost identical characters crossed through, these are for the Malaya POW Book (the smaller crossed through ones above them remain a mystery.).

Above the box is the character for *Thailand* and the Roman numeral II, which indicates Jack was transferred to Thailand and the Burma – Siam Railway as part of Work Battalion or Camp 2 (We refer to them as Battalions or Parties, the Japanese referred to them as Camps)

140

補 修 欄　Other Informations

昭和/8年　月　日 療作業収容所第Ⅱ 分所ヘ移替ス

昭和20年 8月30日　バンコツクニ於テ 聯合国軍ニ引渡ス

First Line: The date of 17 / 11 / 3, which is the reverse of the English: 3 / 11 / 42 – except that the year is expressed as the Year of Showa, as Hirohito's reign was known; 17 = 1942

The party that left Singapore on that date was O Party under the command of Lt. Cl. F. I. N. McOstrich, ROCS, 18th Division. (This was one of the groups known as the Letter Parties which were transported in 13 Parties of 650 between October 25th and November 6th 1942.)

However, this was not the date (and Party) that Jack left Changi. He in fact left on the 2nd November as part of 'P' Party. The Thailand-Burma Railway Centre have lists of all parties and Jack is listed as leaving on this date, along with hundreds of other Cambridgeshires. The 3rd referred to on the Index Card could have been the day the party left the island.

On the next line the year date 18 = 1943, confirming he is on the Railway as part of Work Battalion or Camp 2.

The last line 20 / 8 / 30 = 30 / 8 / 1945 was the date he was released to the Allied Powers.

Appendix 7
POW Questionnaire and Major David Nelson's Diary

Before departing to Rangoon, Jack was required to complete a liberation questionnaire (opposite).

Below is a transcription of the questionnaire.

Camp or Hospital	Dates	Camp Leader	Detachment or Block Leader (if any)
CHUNGHAI	NOV 42 – JAN 43	COL WILLIAMSON	PARTY
BANKOW	FEB 43 – APRIL 43	CAPT DARBY	1ST CAMBS
106 KM			
NOMAK DAI			
NAKOM PATON	MAY 44 – AUG 44	COL TUESDAY	
LINSON	SEPT 44 – MAY 45	MAJ NELSON	RA
TAMAWAN	MAY – JULY 45	RSM ATKINS	
NEW HARBOUR BANKOK	AUG 45	SM BARLOW	LEICESTERS

Major David Nelson kept a detailed diary during his captivity. He was in charge of a woodcutting group that travelled up the railway on 18th September 1944. Jack is listed as being a member of that group.

5830769	2169	"	HOWES	E.T.	1 Cambs.	
5779222	10726	"	HINSON	H.	R. Norfolk R.	022/1
5775062	3996	"	HART	J.	4 R. Norfolk R.	022/1
6028589	3994	"	HARDING	A.	Suffolk R.	12/1
5830871	2183	"	JACOBSEN	C.H.	2 Cambs.	
5933747	5731	"	JONES	F.D.	2 Cambs.	022/1
5830776	4633	"	JENNINGS	J.	1 Cambs.	
5951309	2217	"	LOVEGROVE	F.	Beds. & Herts.	
5828873	10772	"	LIVEMORE	H.	R. Norfolk R.	
5933354	4719	"	MUSK	W.G.	1 Cambs.	
5988213	2230	"	MARRIOTT	E.	Beds. & Herts.	12/1

142

WRITE IN BLOCK CAPITAL LETTERS IN PENCIL.

No. C.X.2254 .... Rank A.75 .... Surname J.JENNINGS ....

Christian Names JACK ...... Decoration ......

Unit & Corps (abbrev) 1.N.Z. CAMP.D. 18 DIV. ....

Date of Birth 18.7.19 .... Date of Enlistment 28.10.27 ....

Private Address and Telephone No. 49 SUTHERLAND RD. C LA DELL

STARS .... SINGAPORE 15 FEB. ....

Place & Date of Original Capture ......

1. What camps, detachments or hospitals were you in? Give dates and names of the
British Camp Leaders, Detachment (or Block) Leaders, in the case of hospitals, the
Senior Medical Officers.

Camp or Hospital.	Dates.	Camp Leader.	Detachment or Block Leader (if any).
CHANGI	NOV 42 – FEB 43	LT. SOUTHGATE	AAB 17
BANPON	FEB 43 APRIL 43	CAPT BAGGY	1ST CAMBS
TAR KNO			
KANAR SAI		L/C BENTLEY	
NACOM PATON	APRIL 43 MAY 43	MAJ. MALLOW	B No
SAIGON	JANUARY 45	ADJ APRIMS	
FRENCH IND		1ST HARLEY	A.E.I.I.GUEGA)

2. ESCAPE (to be completed overleaf). (Additional paper supplied on request if required.)
(a) Give full description and approx. date of each attempt you made to escape,
showing how you left the camp, and from which camp each attempt was made. State
whether there was an escape in progress at the time or not. If an escape was
made from a train or vehicle the approx. speed and how it was guarded should be
included.

(b) Were you physically fit when you made these attempts? ......

(c) Give Regimental particulars of anyone who accompanied you on each attempt.

...... What happened to them?

(d) Give briefly your experiences during periods of freedom.

(e) How were you recaptured and on what date? ....

nil

P.T.O.

Appendix 8
Jack's War Timeline

Exact dates are given where documentary evidence is available. Other dates have had to have been estimated.

Date	Jack	Other Events
1939		
June	Conscription.	
3rd Sept		War Declared with Germany.
20th Oct	Reported to Chelmsford Barracks. Posted to Cambridge for 8 weeks.	
December	Posted to Weeting Hall, Brandon, Norfolk.	
1940		
January	Carpenters' Course in London for 6 months (Cumberland Hotel, Highbury Grove).	
1st July	Returned to Brandon, then posted to coastal defences at Happisburgh, Bacton and Sea Palling.	
1st Nov.	Moved to area around Wymondham.	
1941		
1st Jan.	Posted to Galashiels for 3 months.	
5th April	Posted to area around Cannock	
May	Posted to Arbury Park, Stockingford (Coventry/Nuneaton). (*Footnote 1*)	
Sept.	Posted to Whittington Barracks, Lichfield. The King inspected the Battalion during this time.	
28th Oct	Left Liverpool aboard SS Orcades.	
30th Oct	Joined the rest of the fleet at Greenock in Scotland for the journey across the Atlantic to Halifax, Nova Scotia in Canada.	

2nd Nov	In the middle of the Atlantic, the British convoy met up with an American convoy of escort ships that would escort them to Halifax. The British escorts then left the convoy and this job was taken over by the US Navy.	The United States had not joined the war at this stage, so this convoy remained secret.
8th Nov	Arrived in Halifax.	
10th Nov	Departed Halifax, aboard *West Point* . Part of Convoy William Sail 12X.*(Footnote 2)*	
17th Nov	Stopped-over in Trinidad for 2 days	
24th Nov	Crossed Equator.	
7th /8th Dec		Japanese attacked Pearl Harbour and bomb Singapore. They invaded the Malay peninsula. USA entered the war.
9th Dec	Arrived Cape Town.	
13th Dec	Departed Cape Town. *(Footnote 3)*	
21st Dec		The government of Thailand formally allied itself with Japan.
27th Dec	Arrived Bombay Harbour. *(Footnote 4)*	
29th Dec	Disembarked *(Footnote 5)* and posted to Keren Lines, Admednagar – a 150 mile train journey.	
1942		
19th Jan	Departed Bombay. *(Footnote 6)*	British forces continued to retreat south through central Malaya as the Japanese forced a crossing of the river Slim.
29th Jan	Arrived Singapore and disembarked *(Footnote 7)*. Posted to Ketong area of Singapore.	
30th Jan		Remainder of convoy arrives *(Footnote 8)*

145

31st Jan		Allied forces completed their evacuation of Malaya and withdrew to Singapore Island across the causeway with the Japanese only 8 miles away.
1st Feb	Billeted to area around Seletar Aerodrome	
7th Feb		The Japanese launched a feint landing on Pulua Ubin Island to the east of Singapore.
8th Feb		The Japanese landed on the western side of Singapore Island, encountering only minimal resistance.
9th Feb	Took over forward defences at Seletar. HQ Company in 'bomb dump' area of aerodrome.	By dawn the Japanese 5th and 18th Divisions had firmly established themselves on the island and began to advance south-east towards Singapore city.
11th Feb	Departed Seletar and took up a position on *Hill 105*, on the junction of Braddell Road and Thompson Road, just SE of Macritchie Reservoir.	
12th Feb	Moved to the Adam Park area. HQ Company were posted to the 'hutted camp' to the rear of Adam Park.	
13th Feb	Moved forward to cemetery. Then brought back and dug in on eastern corner of Adam Park estate.	
14th Feb	Hill 95 set alight.	Alexandra Hospital Massacre. *(Footnote 9)*
15th Feb	Surrender of Allied forces in Singapore. Interred on tennis courts.	
20th Feb	Moved to Changi. *(Footnote 10).*	

146

May	To River Valley Road Camp. *(Footnote 11)*	
30th Aug - 5th Sept		Selarang Barracks Incident *(Footnote 12)*
Mid Sept	Returned to Changi.	
2nd Nov	Departed Changi as part of 'P' Party, bound for Thailand.	
6th Nov	In transit through Ban Pong.	
9th Nov	Transferred to Kanchanaburi by truck	
10th Nov	Arrived at Chungkai.	
1943		
15th Jan	Transferred to Wang-Lan (overnight), then on to Wang Takhian.	
21st Feb	Transferred to Ban Khao	
22nd Mar	Transferred to Rintin/Lin Thin	
23rd Mar	Evacuated from Rintin, back to Chungkai. Diagnosed with Renal Colic.	
2nd April	Discharged from hospital.	
22nd Aug	Admitted to Chungkai Camp Hospital with tropical ulcer.	
25th Oct		Siam/Burma Railway completed.
1944		
April	Skin grafted.	
28th May	Graft healed and discharged from hospital.	
	Transferred to Nakhon Pathon	
18th Sept	Transferred to Linton as part of a wood cutting team. *See Appendix 7*	
1945		

May	Sent to work on old Thai State Railway in north of country.	
15th Aug		VJ Day - the war with Japan ended.
25th Aug	Jack (Near Uttaradit) received news of end of war via leaflets dropped in the jungle.	
30th Aug	Jack was officially 'released' by the Japanese – although guards stayed with him for part of the journey south.	
2nd Sept	Evacuation commenced: to Bangkok via Lopburi (2 nights)....	Formal surrender ceremony was performed in Tokyo Bay, Japan aboard the battleship USS Missouri
4th Sept	....to Pratchai (on outskirts of Bangkok).	
8th Sept	Flew to Rangoon.	
20th Sept	Boarded SS Orduna.	
	Sailed via Colombo and Aden.	
8th Oct	Sailed through Suez Canal.	
19th Oct	Arrived Liverpool.	
20th Oct	Disembarked and returned home.	
22nd Dec	Married to Mary.	
1946		
19th April	Demobbed.	

Footnotes to Timeline

1. Whilst based at Arbury Park, the Battalion trained as far afield as Wales and the North Yorkshire Moors.

2. The *West Point* was a converted ocean liner originally named *SS America*. It was built in 1940 for the United States Lines, acquired by the US Navy in 1941 and converted into a troop transport. Cabins meant for four held eight passengers. Lounges, cinemas and gyms became berthing spaces, the cots separated by clothes hanging from lines. Even the large inside swimming pools were drained and converted into dormitories. About 3,250 troops were transported on a ship originally designed to carry 543 in cabin class, 418 in tourist class, 241 in third class, and 643 crew.

CONVOY WILLIAM SAIL 12X
Front Line Top to Bottom
USS West Point - USS Mount Vernon - USS Wakefield
- USS Quincy (Heavy Cruiser)
Back Row Top To Bottom
USAT Leonard Wood - USS Vincennes (Heavy Cruiser)
- USS Joseph T Dickman
Aircraft: Scout Bomber – from USS Ranger (Aircraft Carrier) which was
flying an Anti Submarine patrol over the convoy.
(Other Troop Ship not pictured: USS Orziba)

3.   *West Point* and *Wakefield* were detached to form Task Group (TG) 14.1, while *Leonard Wood* and *Joseph T. Dickman* formed TG 14.2.

4.   TG 14.1, escorted by the *Dorsetshire*, progressed uneventfully towards Bombay until 0700 hours on the 27th, when *West Point* and *Wakefield*, on orders from the British port authorities, increased speed to 20 knots and left the pack to arrive at Bombay at 1600 hours, December 27th. At 1900 hours the *Wakefield* moored at Ballard pier and commenced discharging troops and equipment.

5.   The *West Point* anchored in the harbour until *Wakefield* completed unloading on the 28th. This completed, she anchored out and *West Point* went to Ballard pier at 1615 hours on the 29th

6.   Due to prevailing low-water conditions at Bombay at this point, *West Point* could not go alongside piers in the harbour to either load equipment or troops. Thus, the embarkation and loading procedures had to be carried out by the tedious process of embarking troops and loading supplies from smaller ships

149

and lighters brought alongside. *Wakefield* embarked all the troops which she had brought from Halifax, a total of 4,506, while *West Point* embarked two-thirds of the troops which she had transported, in addition to some which had come out in other ships. All told, she carried some 5,272 men.

In addition to the two American ships, three British transports — *Duchess of Bedford, Empress of Japan,* and *Empire Star* — made up the convoy. Escorted by British light cruiser *HMS Caledon* until this ship was relieved by light cruiser *HMS Glasgow* on January 22, the convoy's escort soon swelled to three cruisers and four destroyers as the convoy neared Java. Japanese submarine activities near the Indonesian archipelago prompted concern for the safe arrival of the valuable ships, hence a 200-mile (320km) detour through the shallow, coral-studded Sunda Strait, led by British cruiser *HMS Exeter.*

7. On the 29th the escort commander suggested that the *West Point, Wakefield* and *Empress of India* leave the convoy, increase speed and proceed to Singapore via Berthala Straits, Durian Strait and Philips channel. The ships steamed through these waters in a bright moonlit night that made navigational aids unnecessary. Upon arrival off Singapore, the ships 'lie-to' in an exposed position, beyond the range of shore based anti-aircraft guns until pilots could bring the ships to Keppel Harbour. The Naval base was now receiving a pounding from the air.

8. On January 30th at about 0935 hours seven Japanese bombers were sighted over the city, and were immediately attacked by British 'Buffalo' fighters. While the fighters were trying to stop the enemy bombers a large formation was reported headed for the transports. Bombs straddled the *West Point* and *Wakefield* until finally *Wakefield* took a bomb hit which exploded in one of her holds, and killed five men. A small tanker alongside Wakefield also took a direct hit and sank. *West Point* sent fire aid parties to help in the treatment of nine crewmen who were injured on *Wakefield.* Despite this, all the troops managed to get ashore by 1800 hours.

9. At about 1pm on 14 February, Japanese soldiers advanced towards the Alexandra Barracks Hospital. A British lieutenant—acting as an envoy with a white flag—approached the Japanese forces but was bayoneted and killed. After the Japanese troops entered the hospital, a number of patients, including those undergoing surgery at the time, were killed along with doctors and members of nursing staff. The following day about 200 male staff members and patients who had been assembled and bound the previous day, many of them walking wounded, were ordered to walk about 400m to an industrial area. Anyone who fell on the way was bayoneted. The men were forced into a series of small, badly ventilated rooms and were imprisoned overnight without water. Some died during the night as a result of their treatment. The remainder were bayoneted the following morning.

10. Following the fall of Singapore, the Japanese military detained about 3,000 civilians in Changi Prison, which was built to house only 600 prisoners. The

Japanese used a number of the British Army's Barracks near the prison as POW camps, holding some 50,000 Allied soldiers. Although POWs were rarely, if ever, held in the civilian prison, the name Changi became synonymous in the UK, Australia, and elsewhere with the POW camp.

11. From *Singapore Heritage Trails Web Site*: The area that is bounded by River Valley Road and Havelock Road was once the site of at least two Prisoner-Of-War (POW) camps during the Japanese Occupation. Named after these two roads, the Havelock Road and River Valley Road Camps were believed to have been referred to interchangeably.

    Prior to the Japanese invasion, the location was a swamp where the British constructed makeshift huts that could easily be evacuated in the event of aerial bombing. By the time the Japanese took control of Singapore in 1942, some accounts noted that the two camps were only separated by a small river or canal with a bridge built across it.

    Once containing up to a total of 5,000 POWs, these camps acted as despatch sites for POW work parties. Their tasks involved the cleaning up and repairing of war-torn parts of the city and the badly bombed Chinatown area.

    The POWs lived in dilapidated attap huts about a hundred feet long with wooden sleeping platforms that could accommodate up to 150 POWs. There was once a Roman Catholic Chapel and also a small library consisting of books collected from some of the houses near the camps. Unknown to the Japanese, there was a radio secretly hidden by the POWs on the grounds, which provided them with news from the outside world. Havelock Road and River Valley Road Camps also had the unusual distinction of running a Masonic Lodge but this ended when numerous POWs were sent to the Death Railway.

12. The *Selarang Barracks Incident* started on 30 August 1942. After the Japanese recaptured four escaped Allied POWs, the Selarang Barracks POWs refused to sign a pledge not to escape, and were forced to crowd in the areas around the barracks square for nearly five days with little water and no sanitation. The executions of the recaptured POWs failed to break the men. The commanders however finally capitulated on September 5 when their men started to fall ill and die from dysentery. Upon signing the pledge, the men were allowed to return to the barracks buildings.

23141115R00090

Printed in Great Britain
by Amazon